JY

STANLEY BALDWIN

STANLEY BALDWIN

KENNETH YOUNG

INTRODUCTION BY
A. J. P. TAYLOR

WEIDENFELD AND NICOLSON
LONDON

Designed by Behram Kapadia
for Weidenfeld and Nicolson Ltd

ISBN 0 297 77100 0

Printed and bound in Great Britain by
Morrison & Gibb Ltd, London and Edinburgh

CONTENTS

ILLUSTRATIONS

INTRODUCTION

'PRIME MINISTER, you. Good Lord!' Such according to Max Beerbohm's cartoon, was the exclamation of Baldwin's Harrovian Young Self when confronted with Baldwin, the pipe-smoking Prime Minister. Such indeed is the initial verdict on Baldwin's career. Of all Prime Ministers Baldwin was the most unexpected. He went into politics reluctantly; he was for years an unassuming backbencher; even during the Great War he occupied only a modest ministerial position. He became a giant killer much to his surprise. Anticipating defeat, he challenged Lloyd George and overthrew the Man who Won the War. A few months later he eclipsed the glittering Marquis Curzon and became Conservative Prime Minister. Thereafter he was often threatened. He was frequently on the verge of being relegated to the obscurity of his Worcestershire home. But he survived his many perils and retired in glory after setting his stamp on the interwar years

Baldwin was a lazy man. He rarely read the papers that were submitted to him by zealous civil servants. He disliked action and would not have been sorry to be remembered as the do-nothing Prime Minister. In one sphere he was assiduous. No Prime Minister has spent longer in the House of Commons. He understood the members of parliament and claimed, perhaps also justifiably, to understand the British people. He was the representative figure of a period when the British had lost their self-confidence.

Baldwin presented himself as a simple countryman, though he actually spent more of his vacations in Aix-les-Bains than in Worcestershire. Beneath his rustic exterior there was a man of infinite guile. Lloyd George was only the first who fell before him. He made Churchill harmless and then impotent throughout the interwar years. He outwitted Beaverbrook with the greatest of ease. He held Neville Chamberlain firmly in the second place. He even dethroned a Monarch. Most of all perhaps he brought Labour within the pale of the constitutional system. Ramsay MacDonald, the Labour leader, became his willing partner. Men will long debate whether he deliberately provoked the general strike. It is certain that he defeated it and yet averted a legacy of bitterness. In foreign affairs, too, his record is disputed. Did he, as Churchill alleged, put party before country? Or did he initiate a policy of deterrence towards Hitler, which Chamberlain then neglected?

Some things can be set indisputably to his credit. Baldwin more than any other political leader pursued a policy of constitutional concession towards India. The attempt failed, but it is thanks to Baldwin that India achieved her freedom and preserved much of the British political heritage until just the other day. Unwittingly Baldwin prepared the national unity which the British displayed during the Second World War. Despite the dark years of unemployment, he softened the asperities of the class war. His failures and omissions were often exasperating; his patience and tolerance were irresistible. 'Give us peace in our time, O Lord' was the burden of one of his most effective speeches. The phrase enshrined his deepest ambition. He brought peace at home, even if at the price of war abroad. In the last resort, Baldwin was a good man. He left maybe a legacy of neglect. But he also preserved and enhanced the civilized values that have distinguished British politics and the British people.

PREFACE

BALDWIN'S reputation and honour, once so infamously be-
smirched, have been properly restored in such vast biographies as
those by K. Middlemas in collaboration with J. Barnes, by H.
Montgomery Hyde and by Baldwin's second son A. W. Baldwin
(the Third Earl). My much shorter study seeks to portray the un-
usual human being behind the politician who was always more of
a statesman. I am grateful to Mr A. E. B. Owen, the under-
librarian of the Cambridge University Library, where Baldwin's
papers are deposited; to Mr Jeremy Boulton of the National Film
Archive; and to Miss Polly Gray of the BBC Sound Archives. I
have received much help and advice from Baldwin's 'beloved
Tommy Dugdale', now First Baron Crathorne, who read part of
the manuscript; from Viscount Bridgeman, the son of one of
Baldwin's closest friends and colleagues; and above all from my
friend and colleague Dr A. J. P. Taylor, who went far beyond the
call of duty as editor in putting his formidable knowledge at my
disposal though disagreeing with some of my opinions.

K.Y.

I

FORTY YEARS
OUTSIDE POLITICS
1867–1908

MRS ALFRED BALDWIN, pretty in her high-necked bodice and bustle, was twenty-two and expecting her first child. In her fine damson brick Georgian house at Bewdley, near the rushing Severn, she reclined on the chaise-longue, a book of Miss Rossetti's poems in her hand, on her lap a bowl of cherries from which now and then she picked and ate. The summer sun poured through the window and the child within stirred. Then it gave a mighty kick which sent the bowl of cherries spinning from Mrs Baldwin's lap to the floor. The lively child was born a few days later, on the morning of 3 August 1867. It was a boy. Emma, the family cook, bore him up three flights of stairs to the very top of the house and to get as high as possible stood on a chair and raised the baby above her head. This to her superstitious Worcestershire mind made sure that the baby would rise in the world. So he did, to the premiership of England, fifty-six years later, and thirteen years after that to an earldom.

By the time the baby's father, the towering black-bearded Alfred Baldwin, drove back in his dogcart from the family iron-works four miles away at Wilden, rejoicing was in full swing. The happy parents decided to call him Stanley after his paternal great-grandfather, the Rev. Jacob Stanley, Wesleyan Minister of Alnwick in Northumberland. A month later he was christened in the thirteenth century church a mile down the road at Ribbesford.

The Baldwins originated in Shropshire where they had been settled as farmers in Corve Dale since Domesday. In the early

1

years of the Industrial Revolution, some of them moved into Worcestershire and started small forges, worsted spinning mills and a carpet manufactory. They prospered and even acquired profitable collieries in South Wales; then they declined. The year before Stanley's birth they were close to bankruptcy. When Stanley was three his father, Alfred, then twenty-nine, bought out his elder brothers and by business acumen and sheer hard work slowly put the firm back on the path to prosperity, expanded vastly, and twenty years later was chairman of the Great Western Railway, of the Metropolitan Bank and of the Aldridge Colliery Company. He became MP for West Worcestershire.

Looking 'half grandee, half Hebrew prophet', Alfred Baldwin was a most unworldly man of the world. Religion was the mainspring of his life. God entered into every interstice of his daily life. About his every act he argued with himself in his voluminous diaries. He was soundly educated at the Wesleyan Collegiate Institution in Taunton; he read widely and thought deeply and thereby was anguishedly introspective; and within that great physical frame he suffered lifelong agonies of panic anxiety. His nerves, his grandson A. W. Baldwin wrote, 'were so sharp-edged that he was often hard put to it to master them, and his outward gravity in later life was probably due to the naturally rather sombre complexion of his mind and in part to the constant evidence of his beloved wife's uncertain health. This frailty no doubt was the cause of a tendency to twitch his facial muscles, rather in the manner that came to be observed in his son, a trick which, with the aid of a capricious eyeglass, often caused some apprehension to those who did not know him well. One nervous affliction in particular tormented him all his life and that was an abnormal dread of thunderstorms. They reduced him to a low and apprehensive state . . . When the tempest rolled and crashed, this powerful-looking man really suffered pitiably.'

This intensely nervous disposition his son, Stanley, inherited, though it was not evident in his earliest years. He, too, would twitch, snap his fingers, lift blotting-paper to smell it; before quite minor occasions, 'the colour would leave his face, the sweat would roll off his brow and time and again he felt he might be sick'. At the height of his career, waiting to read the lesson at St Andrew's University, he had to use all his powers to stop himself 'leaving the place from sheer panic nerves'. Stanley fortunately inherited, too, his father's enormous powers of will and self-control along with his devoutness and intelligence.

Stanley's mother was a being from an altogether different world. While the Baldwins were English for generations back, Louisa, née Macdonald, was a mixture of Highland Scottish, Irish and Welsh ancestry. Stanley, when he was grown up, used to say that 'the odd, erratic creature which is me is caused by the Celtic mixture', and it may account for his mysticism and his moments of clairvoyance. He sometimes told how 'my mother's family fled from the Highlands after having been out with Prince Charles in 1745' or, embroidering a little: 'I remember that in my early days it was with great difficulty that we could stand up while the band was playing God Save the King because we had a Hanoverian and not a Jacobite King.' Stanley's mother was the daughter of a Wesleyan Minister who, though penurious, imbued his family with the true Scottish passion for education. They loved and practised the arts but they were also witty and they laughed a lot. All the four daughters were gifted. Louisa published four romantic novels, poems, tales for children and 'The Shadow on the Blind, and other Ghost Stories'. One of her sisters was to be the mother of Rudyard Kipling; another married the gentle Edward Burne-Jones, the Pre-Raphaelite artist; and a third became the wife of the painter Edward Poynter, afterwards President of the Royal Academy. Stanley as a boy lived in a family circle of doers in the arts. When he stayed with his Poynter cousins, his uncle taught him how to mix paints on a palette and he allowed Stanley to add a brush stroke or two to his masterpiece, 'Atalanta's race'. At the Burne-Jones's he listened to the Rossettis, Swinburne and William Morris gossiping about their work and, of course, politics.

At home, however, Stanley was often lonely, for he remained an only child. Moreover his mother and father loved each other with passion and were absorbed in each other to such an extent that they 'felt it needful to caution each other to be particularly tender towards Stanley lest he might think himself a stranger – such was their love and devotion'. His mother, too, was not always available. Shortly after Stanley's birth she developed an undiagnosed illness which made walking difficult. She had to spend much time lying in a room with the blinds drawn and when she went into the garden it was in a wheel-chair. She sought treatment at various European spas but her health was not restored until Stanley was sixteen. Of course there were brief intervals of boyish fun and games when, for instance, he and his cousin Rudyard enjoyed a gleeful holiday on an Essex farm which they were still talking about forty years later; or when another cousin, Ambrose Poynter, came on one of his 'wild visits'. Stanley was spoken of as droll and affectionate with, however, a temper which he tensely controlled. Once, when he was seven, a great commotion broke out, with Ambrose shouting ever more shrilly and Stanley's voice growing lower and lower. 'Why don't you speak louder, Stan?' screamed Ambrose, to which Stan whispered: 'Because if I spoke any louder I should hit you.'

Stanley's more habitual companions were books. He early absorbed Scott, Malory, Bunyan, *Pickwick*, *Alice*, and Elizabethan history. He dowsed himself in history. Perhaps this is why he saw in the gallery of the local church, during a Sunday service, Queen Elizabeth, Raleigh and Essex – he knew they were Elizabethans, he said, because they wore ruffs. For more formal studies a tutor visited him on certain days in the week, teaching him English, Latin, French and maths, as well as music and drawing. When he was nine his father reported him 'busily engaged in writing his French Revolution!' Physical recreation was confined, because of his solitariness, to skating in the winter, pony-riding and tramping the lanes, sometimes declaiming to himself 'The Lay of the Last Minstrel' or 'Marmion'. Often he would stop and stare over the horizon to the distant hills with their windy crests, the sight of which in later years was to bring him solace and spiritual healing.

The Baldwin family had moved in 1870 from Bewdley to Wilden where the forge and offices were. Stanley's father was a true father to his work people, in whose hearts his memory was cherished for half a century after his death, and he wanted to live among them. The new home lay just across the lane from the forge where the steam-hammers thumped; when the wind was from the west, its grit and smoke blew into the windows of Wilden House. Attached to it was a home farm where Stanley sometimes strolled, asking the manager questions about the animals and agricultural processes. The Baldwin works, as so often in those days, were set in a smiling, pastoral landscape. Around Wilden, rural lanes meandered, orchards blossomed and in the autumn the scent of hops and cider mingled with the acrid fumes from the forge. Alfred Baldwin paid little heed either to the landscape or the fumes; he drove ever forward, despite many setbacks, to make his business succeed, and gradually he did. They had long been gentry; now they were gentry with rising expectations. As such, their only son must follow the gentry's example and be despatched to a preparatory boarding-school, the sort of school which neither his father nor his grand-father had attended.

So when Stanley was ten he travelled with his father and mother to Slough in Buckinghamshire where he entered recently-founded Hawtrey's. His parents, dreading the parting, left him with a parcel of books and much advice: 'You can't always be top but always be top if you can; stick to work and to cricket,' said his mother. His father wrote: 'You were a very good, brave boy this afternoon and I was very pleased with your manly way. If you will be as good in your work and as brave in your play, you will indeed do well.' Stanley obeyed. He played football as well as cricket and was in all things quick – a slim, fair-haired boy with blue eyes and reddish eyebrows. He came top of the school and won eighteen prizes but, to his own and his father's dismay, when he was thirteen he had examination nerves and failed his Harrow scholarship. He never spoke of the failure, much less of the 'nerves' that caused it.

So it was as an ordinary fee-paying pupil that he arrived at Harrow in 1881 and was put in the House of the headmaster, Dr Montague Butler, a well-known pedagogue. At first he did well, was picked for the house football XI when he was fifteen, enjoying cricket and playing a vigorous game of squash. He won form prizes for history and mathematics and was adept at the classics. His letters home suggest a mild interest in politics, naturally enough since his father was always being asked to stand for Parliament though he did not do so until 1892. It was only after Stanley him-self entered politics that he recalled that, while his father voted Whig in the 1868 election, 'I wore the Tory colours in my pram . . . our cook was a Tory and she saw to that'. Politics did not truly interest Stanley at Harrow; it was the grown man who talked of being born in the year which 'saw two symbolic things happen – the publication of Marx's *Capital* with its gospel of economic fatalism, and Disraeli's extension of the franchise to working men, with its faith in expanding freedom'.

Stanley reached the fifth form at Harrow, a promising boy. Then the welkin split open. The headmaster sent off a telegram to Wilden House summoning his father to the school; Stanley had composed a piece of pornography (whose exact nature is not clear) and, what was worse, had sent a copy of it to his cousin Ambrose at Eton. Alfred Baldwin, whatever his inner dismay, was surprisingly calm. Having listened to the headmaster's story, he wrote home to Louisa: 'The whole affair was much exaggerated and far more folly than anything else ... the upshot is a flogging, which is now over and done with.' The flogging, yes; Dr Butler was known to birch but lightly and during the operation to comfort the culprit with such expressions as 'Please be brave' and 'It hurts me so'. The aftermath, however, was serious. It caused a breakdown of relations between Stanley and the headmaster; he was not given the monitorship he expected when he reached the Upper Sixth; he lost interest in work and assumed the bovine, indolent mask which he put on in later life when he was bored and frustrated. From then on he did a modicum of study. Forty years later he was still rationalizing his laziness at school. At a dinner of the Harrow Association on 19 July 1923, he said: 'Thanks be to Heaven, there is in every English boy an unconscious but impregnable resistance to every form of pressure made by any schoolmaster who works him too hard or tries to put too much inside him. I know that was so in my case ...' This resistance ensured that the boys' bodies could grow undisturbed by mental storms until they got into their early twenties and 'able to graft the sane mind on the sane body'. The memory of Dr Butler rankled for long, though Stanley would in the end turn it into jest. He told a public audience later that once the great Mr Gladstone addressed the school and he eagerly awaited his message. But 'when Mr Gladstone opened with the words "Your admirable headmaster", I felt that the Prime Minister was so out of touch with the whole of the life I was leading that I never listened to another word'. Later still he even joked about having given up pornography when he left Harrow.

Stanley went up to Trinity College, Cambridge, in 1885, only to learn with a sinking heart that Dr Butler was about to become its Master. He read history; how consistently may be seen from the record: a first in Part One of the Tripos, a second in Part Two, and a third in Finals. 'I hope', wrote his father stingingly, 'you won't get a third in life.' Nor was he more active in non-academic pursuits. Elected to the college debating society, the Magpie and Stump, he was asked to resign because he never spoke. He was afterwards to remark jauntily: 'I attribute such faculties as I have to the fact that I did not overstrain them in youth,' but by 1924 he could admit to being ashamed of wasting so much time at the university, particularly because, he ventured to think, he had 'the capacity to take advantage' of his chances – 'these things come home to us as we get older'. Whether his poor showing at Cambridge was due to the arrival of Dr Butler or to his having habituated himself to laziness cannot now be discovered.

In the middle of his undergraduate career Stanley suffered a shock so awful that he never spoke of it in later life. His sports-loving cousin Harold had been taken into the bosom of the Wilden Baldwins after the death of his father, Alfred Baldwin's elder brother, and Wilden became his home. He was the same age as Stanley and had gone up to Cambridge with him, but to Pembroke not Trinity. They were great friends. One fine morning in spring 1886 Stanley was called over to Pembroke. Harold had fallen out of his bedroom window and broken his leg. In hospital it was discovered that he was a chronic epileptic. He was taken back to Wilden to begin his business career, but over the years fit followed fit and Stanley often witnessed the horrible foamings and writhings. Harold, once the healthy boisterous cousin, eventually retired into the life of a semi-invalid. It was from these years that Stanley began to show the tics and twitches so familiar in his adult life.

Stanley went down from Cambridge in 1888. He told Dr Butler that he was first going into business and then into the House of Commons, which is exactly what he did. But he had toyed with thoughts of the priesthood ('I don't know that I am surprised,' his father wryly commented), and had spent an Easter vacation at the college mission in Camberwell, South London. Though he did not take holy orders, religion and prayer became as much a daily reality to him as it was to his father and mother. Stanley did not talk about it often, though once in 1928 he came out with it fair and square. Speaking of work in politics and in civic life he said: 'If I did not believe that that work was done in faith and hope that some day, it may be a million years hence, the Kingdom of God would spread over the whole world, I could have no hope, I could do no work and I would give my office over this morning to anyone who would take it.'

Meantime he was twenty-one and life was real, life was earnest. He spent a month or two training as an officer in the Artillery Volunteers – he dreaded mess dinners as the officers, his cousin

7

observed, 'are hardly his style' – and then joined his father's business. He was to remain there in a full-time capacity for twenty years. He started at the bottom at £2 a week, working in his father's office at the Wilden Forge. It was not what he wanted to do – but then what *did* he want to do? But he buckled to and within a few months became, according to his cousin Harold, 'quite the man of business when in the office, but once outside the same dear merry soul he has ever been . . . He's almost as keen on it as his father . . . he's wonderfully quick and grasps a situation in no time.' Though, he added, 'at the same time from the bottom of his heart he detests it'. The job was what Stanley needed, giving him back the discipline, responsibility and the habit of hard work which he had lost at Harrow and Cambridge. 'For twenty years he lived by the clock until punctuality and the doing of the work of the day became an unshakeable habit.' He learned to read balance-sheets quickly, he assimilated the whole paraphernalia of business and developed a shrewd judgement.

The firm's expansion, particularly during the 1890s, was partly a result of a managerial reorganization, partly of Baldwin's considerable administrative gift and his ability to get on with people, not least with the workmen. He knew every man, could talk with them about their troubles whether at work or at home. Strikes and lock-outs were unknown at E. P. & W. Baldwins over three generations. No one got the sack and 'a large number of old gentlemen used to spend their days sitting on the handles of wheelbarrows, smoking their pipes', he recalled. When a coal strike threw them out of employment in 1912, the company paid them an allowance. Many were Baldwin's gifts and stealthy charity to his men. Of course he foresaw that, though his was 'not an inefficient community' – though they were still smelting with charcoal in 1900 – it would eventually be swallowed up in the inevitable amalgamations towards which industry was tending. Baldwins became a public company, amalgamated with three firms (including a Welsh colliery in 1902), and by the early years of the twentieth century the combine was dealing with all the stages in the production of iron and steel, from the raw materials to tin-plate and galvanized sheets.

Baldwin visited his company's associates in Canada and the United States, and learned another fact of industrial life – that the introduction of the McKinley tariff in 1890–1 would severely damage British sales in America; indeed within a few years all his company's American market was lost. Baldwin knew what he was talking about when he later espoused a tariff policy: Britain's much vaunted Free Trade was, as far as the USA, Japan and Germany were concerned, free in only one direction. Baldwin was aware that the tariff barriers were not the only cause of Britain's declining exports. Her industrial equipment was obsolescent, her technological education far behind that of Germany and the United States. Instead of training men as managers, industry relied too much on 'practical' men who had come up the hard way. Baldwins was a case in point, but the young master himself was not disposed to do much about it; the paternalistic bond held him no less than his father. Once, half-heartedly, he allowed a firm of costing and management experts into the Wilden works. The experts discovered that the average intelligence of the workmen was only 30 per cent of the normal. 'Well', said Baldwin, 'you couldn't expect an average intelligence of more than that. I don't see why you should.'

At the forge Baldwin wore baggy riding breeches and gaiters; when he visited subsidiary companies, or went to the metal exchanges, or spoke at meetings in his father's constituency of West Worcestershire (for which Alfred sat from 1892), he put on morning coat and striped trousers. But it was not all work. There were weekend tennis parties, long and even longer walks in the hills (where he carried wire-cutters to preserve rights-of-way), village cricket in the summer, skating in the winter, singing *basso decani* in the Wilden Church choir on Sundays and playing the piano. He read as compulsively as when he was a boy, poetry in particular. Such voracious reading was not thought natural for a man of his age and occupation. At a weekend party, when he was discovered reading a book, he was asked: 'Got the hump, old man?' He was not a bookworm; he was always ready to take part in any sort of ball game, including football with his workmen. He seems not to have played golf; he neither hunted nor shot nor fished, though he was once seen riding in Rotten Row.

In this spring of his days he never walked where he could run; he leaped over everything in his path, sofas, tables and armchairs. Flights of stairs were taken at a bound and even when he was first in Downing Street twenty years later he mounted the steps two at a time and at the double. He was great fun at family parties but

9

he never cared for grand receptions. In fact, his younger daughter, Margaret, recalled that 'he was terrified of big receptions and always tried to keep near the wall in case the floor gave way!' He disliked the boisterousness of society males on their own at stag nights or after Hunt Balls, 'the horse of British aristocracy baying for broken glass,' in Evelyn Waugh's words. He was rather abstemious. With women he was not at ease. Sometimes, he wrote in his early twenties, 'I thought I was making a modest success on my own but I have never made any real impression on a woman. I may have had a modest success for an evening if the party was particularly dull, but to be remembered next day, much less next week, never.'

Then, on a visit to his Burne-Jones relations at Rottingdean, near Brighton, he was introduced to the formidable Ridsdale family. The father, Edward Ridsdale, a former Master of the Mint, was a scientist, an agnostic and a Liberal. His three sons and two daughters were noisy, games-playing, and extrovert. Baldwin began a slow, quiet courtship of the elder daughter, Cissy (her real name was Lucy) after, it was said, watching her score a half-century in a ladies' cricket match. When he was twenty-five, they were married at Rottingdean on 12 September 1892. He was attracted to Cissy, he wrote to his mother, because of 'her absolute innocence and unworldliness and the strong loyalty she felt towards every member of her own family'. She was forthright, jolly, party-loving and, as a wife, infinitely protective towards those aspects of Baldwin's nature that so differed from her own – his mysticism and need for solitude, his love of the arts. She did not share his long ruminative walks for which he chose such other companions as Phyllis Broome, a Worcestershire neighbour. But it was Cissie who, when Baldwin faltered, urged him, 'Go on, Tiger,' and she was the real trigger to his latent political ambition. Stanley and Cissy were in some ways opposites. She was Low Church, he High Anglican, no matter then for easy dismissal. She was brisk and organizing, party-loving and an enthusiast for good causes. Something of the schoolgirl lived on in her. Innocently, at a fund-raising gathering to help unmarried mothers, she convulsed her audience by saying with much *empressement*: 'I want every one of you in this audience to be responsible for at least one unmarried mother.' She and Stanley lived together, seldom separated, in love and amity for over half a century.

Their first child was still-born but later came two sons and three daughters. These were the happy, private years, and prosperous, too. Though mostly they stayed in West Worcestershire they took many holidays, staying with friends in Britain and extensively exploring Europe – France, the Italian lakes, Vienna, Berlin, Dresden, Munich, Salzburg; in the middle of January, most years, they were to be found at winter sports centres, often with the Kiplings. Baldwin skied energetically if not stylishly. It was the Alpine scenery that most deeply impressed him as much for its spiritual as for its scenic quality: 'I don't know any environment on this earth that brings me more into tune with unseen things,' he wrote. Baldwin in the years before 1914 had much more than a tourist's acquaintance with Western Europe, particularly since he spoke, read and wrote French fluently and had passable German. On the whole he liked Europeans but he could be a little choosy about his fellow-countrymen he met abroad: 'I don't much care for the kind of people in this hotel,' he once wrote to his mother, 'they ain't my style.'

The Baldwins moved in 1902 to the honey-coloured, gabled Astley Hall above the Severn, south of Stourport and facing Abberley Hill: this was their home for the rest of their lives. The estate was some hundred acres with tenant farms. Year by year the Hall garden was extended and embellished under the guidance of Cissy Baldwin. On the home farm a few cows, some pigs and poultry were kept, although the mechanics of farming Baldwin left to his wife and the cowman. But he 'really did like leaning over a gate and scratching a pig,' wrote J. C. C. Davidson, later his colleague and firmest friend in the political years. He liked still more talking to farmers and farm labourers. 'He was the son of an industrialist and ran an ironworks, but it was really the land which he came from, the oldest and biggest industry of all', on which generations of his Baldwin ancestors had worked.

Life at Astley was cushioned by eight indoor servants, a butler, ten gardeners and a chauffeur; later came a housekeeper to relieve Cissy of some of her duties when she was 'low, slack' or suffering from neuralgia. Baldwin was a man of consequence though he neither felt it nor showed it. It was a firm sense of duty, not the desire for local prominence, that led him to sit on the parish council and Worcestershire County Council, to serve as a magistrate and as chairman of the Wilden school managers. He helped canvass his father's parliamentary constituency, stopping in many a bar parlour to drink cider and smoke a pipe with the locals; he was a member of such bodies as the Foresters and Oddfellows.

His father always hoped that Stanley might join him in the House of Commons, and a chance came in 1904 when the sitting member for Kidderminster announced that he would not be standing at the next election. Baldwin was adopted. He had often listened to debates in the Commons and met his father's friends, such as Joseph Chamberlain, his son Austen, Chancellor of the Exchequer, and Bonar Law who was, at forty-four, Parliamentary Secretary to the Board of Trade. All three were Tariff Reformers; no one exactly knew what Prime Minister Balfour was since his ever more onerous task was to keep the Tariff Reformers and the Free Traders in his Cabinet together. When it became impossible – and there was also a chance to exploit the divisions among the Liberals – Balfour resigned and a General Election was to take place in January 1906.

Baldwin opened his campaign on a wet night in a Kidderminster school soon after Christmas 1905. He preached tariff reform: 'How can we secure the necessary employment as long as we expose our own labour to the unrestricted competition of the labour of the world by admitting into our markets the products of the cheapest Continental and Eastern labour?' He inveighed against Home Rule for Ireland, the secularization of the schools and the disestablishment of the Welsh Church. His chairman referred to him as 'a plain, straightforward man', a persona that Baldwin was to adopt. Kidderminster, however, was far from a straightforward constituency; there was a smell of corruption about its elections. Nor were certain aspects of the electioneering required of him to Baldwin's taste. While he enjoyed dropping into country pubs, he was expected to spend three evenings a week in one of the many large hostelries, there vociferously to applaud what 'for want of a better name, was called ... comic and humorous song'. After 'these orgies I felt in need of a moral purge and a literal sedative'. So before he went to bed he read the *Odyssey*, the *Aeneid* and all the Odes of Horace ('not without labour in the dictionaries') with the desired result that 'I had passed through the fire and the smell of burning was not on my garments'. It reads priggishly; it was much more the fastidiousness that made him recoil from officers' mess 'dining-in nights' and the British abroad.

Baldwin was defeated at Kidderminster. In that election it was nearly impossible for any Tory not to be; Balfour himself lost his seat and the party reassembled in the Commons was a pathetic 157 all told, while Labour suddenly began to be taken notice of with its fifty-three seats. Baldwin's father, himself re-elected, was deeply cast down by his son's defeat; was it for him Cambridge all over again? Stanley Baldwin was more depressed by his father's depression than at his own failure. He himself was not yet fired by the thought of being an MP. He took himself off for two days walking in the Cotswolds, returning 'a new man and purged of my humours'. Soon afterwards, Worcester City fell vacant as a result of the newly elected member being unseated for corrupt practices. But the writ was suspended for a year and – a new disappointment – when it was moved an Irishman, Edward Goulding (later Lord Wargrave), was adopted. Baldwin was almost forty; there need be no General Election before 1913 (Parliaments then lasted seven years) and he felt that it would be almost too late then to start as an MP. There, but for his wife and father, his political career might have ended before it had properly begun. 'If it hadn't been for my mother', wrote Baldwin's daughter Margaret, 'my father would have remained quite happily where he was in Worcestershire ... He had had no ambition, push or drive. My mother supplied them all.'

A tragic irony now intervened to make sure that Britain should have one of her most successful premiers. Alfred Baldwin suddenly died in London on 13 February, 1908, which shocked and grieved his family and the many friends who so highly regarded him. His father's old constituents asked Stanley Baldwin to take his place; out of respect to his father the Liberals forbore to put up a candidate, which was again a stroke of luck, for he would not in the midst of his grief have contemplated campaigning. Completely without confidence in his ability to play his new role, he left for London far from certain that he should care for living there half the year. 'I am sure', he said, 'that Hell is full of electric trams tearing about and getting nowhere.'

2

INTO THE SPIDER'S WEB
1908–1922

BALDWIN was introduced into the House of Commons at a quarter to four on 6 March 1908, striding up to Mr Speaker between Austen Chamberlain and Michael Hicks Beach. Some Members who had known his father hastened to welcome him, this pleasant-looking, sandy-haired man of medium height with the firm chin and pale blue eyes, who now sat down on the back benches and sniffed his order paper. There he was to sit, sometimes looking a little bovine, sometimes following a debate with lively interest, for almost ten years, seldom speaking – six times in the six years up to 1914 – but assiduous in committee work, in answering constituents' letters, in speaking at by-elections.

He rose to make his maiden speech near dinner-time, when the Chamber was almost empty, on 22 June 1908. He spoke for twenty minutes on the Liberal Government's Bill to limit work in coal mines to eight hours a day. He opposed it. He was, he told the House, head of a firm which long ago had given one section of their employees an eight-hour day, so he might be acquitted of being constitutionally against working men. But the result of the Bill would be too far-reaching; it would raise the price of coal, which, in turn, would have a devastating effect on industry and would price exports out of the markets. The rich and prosperous Miners' Union would benefit at the expense of other workers less fortunately circumstanced. Thence would come a general demand for higher wages, in a time of falling trade; and the coal trade itself, would be plunged into a serious state of strife. He objected, too, to the Government being given, in a clause to the Bill, the right to

14

interfere in cases of great economic disturbance; that was too much power to put into the hands of any government. He sat down and went home and wrote to his mother: 'I thought the speech a poor one, it was a deadly experience.' But anywhere and everywhere, he added, he felt his father's spirit with him; he vividly expected to meet him again, 'where or in what shape I know not', and perhaps to do something that would earn from him a 'well done'.

Baldwin lived in London in a fine house in Queen's Gate, South Kensington, which he exchanged in 1913 for an even finer one in Eaton Square. He was very prosperous as vice-chairman and executive head of the now large conglomerate known as Baldwins Ltd. He joined clubs and bought pictures (nothing later than 1900) and went to concerts at the Queen's Hall. He and his wife entertained and were in turn entertained by such Conservatives as Eyres Monsell, Spender Clay, Locker Lampson, W. A. S. Hewins, director of the London School of Economics, and Austen Chamberlain. They saw much of the Kiplings, and the Mackails one of whom became the novelist Angela Thirkell; they were at Astley in the summer, Switzerland in the winter, in London only half the year.

To Baldwin as yet politics was a hobby; probably, he thought, gazing on the great men of the Commons – Asquith, Grey, Churchill, Lloyd George – it would never be more, for he did not believe he could ever emulate them. Even in his own much depleted party, could he deploy the suavity and intellect of Balfour, restored to Parliament after a by-election in the City of London, or the toughness of Law, or the brilliant speech of the young F. E. Smith? 'It is difficult work making one's way in a place like the House of Commons,' he told his mother. 'Keep pounding at 'em is the only thing.' He did not tell her his doubt whether he even wanted to make his way, but desultorily he 'pounded' away, and gradually came to have a feeling for the Commons and its ways and moods.

He would never be a whole-hearted, my-party-right-or-wrong MP. He was one of only twelve Conservatives who spurned the whips and voted for the Government's Old Age Pensions Bill. On the other hand he had the businessman's distrust of the Government's massive social legislation: 'It ought to be an integral part of a statesman's duty today, when speaking on a platform, not only to point out to the people the benefits that may accrue to them by expenditure on social legislation, but to point out with equal candour and fairness what the charges will be on the nation for such benefits.' He criticized the famous Lloyd George budget of 1909, with its increased death duties, its new supertax and its steep rise in land value duties, but not on the diehard ground which was to precipitate a constitutional crisis. He was against it because he was sure that high taxation was not the answer to the stagnation that had fallen over industry. What was needed was 'such steps to protect trade that will increase the amount available for wages ... to make money filter through to the people', not the stirring up of 'envy and hatred of the poorer people against the richer people ... not by threatening industry and despoiling individuals'. He spoke of the Chancellor, Lloyd George, as 'wandering in a sort of Celtic twilight among figures'.

For a long time Baldwin felt most at home not in the Chamber but in the smoking-room, where he would sit and puff his briar-root pipe, half leaning towards one or another group. He liked talking with the working-men MPs in the Labour party; he had the same *rapport* with them as with his own workmen at Wilden. He had no party bias. He chatted on the friendliest basis with such men as the bluff but shrewd J. H. Thomas, the railwaymen's leader discussing means of collective bargaining between industry and the unions; the I.L.P., however, struck him as 'too intellectual'. In the Chamber itself Baldwin gradually gained confidence, sometimes even bringing off an epigram. 'It is one thing to do good to your soul by renouncing your own earthly goods, but it is quite another to do good to another man's soul by taking away his goods.' His voice was firm and agreeable and he spoke in direct conversational style, seldom drifting into lazy abstractions and far from the rodomontade of Lloyd George and others. He did not want to be an orator; he would try and try again 'to say what I really think'. This did not go unremarked. Unknown to Baldwin there was an occasion during one of his speeches when Asquith, the Prime Minister, whispered to Simon, the Solicitor-General, 'Do you notice what good English this man talks?' and asked who he was.

Baldwin, who had stepped unopposed into his father's seat, had to fight a Liberal in the General Election of January 1910, which the Government demanded to break the power of the Lords, who had rejected their budget. Tariff reform was not a real issue, though Baldwin campaigned as 'a Tariff Reformer who would prefer to raise revenue by taxing foreign imports rather than by increasing the heavy taxes already existing on tobacco, liquor and land.' On the actual issue of the election, he wrote in his election address: 'The Radical party wish to take away the power of the House of Lords in order to facilitate the passage of a Home Rule Bill [for Ireland] knowing that this is a policy which for twenty years the people of England have refused to support.' Wearing their red rosettes, then the Tory colours in the west, Baldwin and his wife in their decorated car toured Spetchley and Claines and Ombersley and Hallow, sipping warm cider in bar parlours, 'though my thrifty soul begrudges the money'. They were rewarded. Baldwin added 4,248 votes to the majority he had inherited. In the country at large the Liberal majority over the Tories sank to two; now the Irish Nationalists with eighty-two seats and Labour with forty held the balance of power. A second election the same year of 1910 had a similar result.

The Government, tight within the irksome grip of Redmond's Irish Nationalists, grew frustrated, party relations were embittered and a sort of frenzy seized on the political world. There was the Marconi shares scandal, which added a dimension to Baldwin's distrust of Lloyd George's demagoguery and financial irresponsibility. (Lloyd George, Sir Rufus Isaacs and the Master of Elibank had bought shares in the American Marconi Company at a time when the British Marconi Company had been given a big government contract to develop an Imperial wireless chain. The shares had been offered them by one of Isaacs's brothers. During a debate on the subject, the three ministers had not declared their interest. A Select Committee exonerated them of dishonesty but Lloyd George and Isaacs apologized in the Commons for their error of judgement.)

Baldwin thought that the affair 'dimmed George's prestige for many a day to come. He looked very vicious when brought to bay and while making his apology'. The other Liberal who was implicated, Rufus Isaacs, was made Lord Justice of England soon afterwards, and Baldwin heard with some pleasure his cousin Kipling's cruel verse diatribe which was passed around from mouth to mouth. The smell of corruption lingered on the air. Kipling's poem, published later, tells how Gehazi, i.e. Isaacs, is made a judge for telling Naaman, i.e. Asquith, that 'all is well', and how when he, Gehazi, having himself 'barely 'scaped from judgement', in taking his judicial vows, he is struck by leprosy. Here is part of the poem:

> Take oath to judge the land
> Unswayed by gift or money
> Or privy bribe, more base,
> Of knowledge which is profit
> In any market place.
>
> Search out and probe Gehazi,
> As thou of all canst try,
> The truthful, well-weighed answer
> That tells the blacker lie . . .

Far more disturbing to Baldwin the industrialist was a rash of strikes on a scale England had never known before. Railwaymen, dockers, boilermakers, miners downed tools, were locked out by employers, rioted, looted and were shot down by troops and police. Two men were killed in Liverpool, two in Llanelly, and more troops were put on stand-by in parks and encampments. Some forty-one million working days were lost in 1912 compared with eleven million the year before. Baldwin spoke in the Commons of his abhorrence of big strikes or big lock-outs: 'I am proud to think that during the twenty years I have been responsible for the management of a large number of men there has never been any question of a lock-out or strike . . . There is a spirit in these modern strikes which if carried on must make more difficult the attainment of that mutual and collective bargaining on which trade unions for so many years, and rightly from their point of view, have insisted.' Baldwin knew but did not add that the 'new spirit' sprang not from the trade-union leadership but from a minority of 'revolutionary syndicalist' agitators infiltrating the unions and determined to use strikes and violence to intimidate Parliament. These strikers of 1910–12 moulded Baldwin's thoughts and, afterwards, his policies towards encouraging the solid centre of the Labour Party and so making them less susceptible to the wild men. He was thinking far ahead of most of his choleric, empurpled colleagues of the Opposition.

Baldwins Limited and in particular E. P. & W. Baldwins were inevitably affected by the strikes. The workers at Wilden did not stop work of their own volition but because the South Wales coal strike cut off the fuel for the forges and steam-hammers. Between them and starvation stood only the Friendly Societies, since un-employment insurance, passed by the Government in 1911, was confined to industries which suffered cyclical worklessness. Baldwin promptly gave allowances to those of his men 'who had been without wages coming in for at least a week'.

The undercurrent of violence alarmed many people and it was reported that one wholesale armourer had sold out of his stock of revolvers. Even the suffragettes, or some of them, took to chaining themselves to railings and attacking policemen, and their demand for the vote turned into an anti-man campaign. The disease of violence was catching. Not only did strikers riot and troops fire on them, but the top-hatted Tories, including their new leader Bonar Law, incited Ulstermen to armed mutiny against the Government's Irish Home Rule Bill. To Baldwin's apalled dismay, Law even gave his blessing to the clandestine smuggling into Larne from Hamburg of 35,000 rifles and three million cartridges for use by Ulster Volunteers against the British army, itself unsure whether or not to remain loyal to the Asquith Government. The pacific Baldwin, unaffected by the mad fever that ran through the veins of so many of his senior colleagues, told his mother: 'There is a move among moderate men on both sides to get together on the Irish question and try to arrange some compromise that will make for peace, the one idea being at any cost to save the country from civil war or from a wild campaign against the army.'

Baldwin added in this same letter of March 1914: 'never in our lives have we been standing on such a perilous brink.' He was right, though it was not the brink of civil war but of war with Germany. It was as great a shock to Baldwin as to most of his fellow countrymen when Britain declared war on 4 August 1914. Neither he nor the majority of back-benchers in the Commons knew much about the conduct of British foreign policy: that was a matter for the experts. The idea of a European war had been talked about for so long that no one really believed it would ever happen. There had been scares over Germany's naval building and there had been the crisis over Agadir. The famous old soldier Lord Roberts had stumped the country demanding 'national service', and he was supported by the great pro-consul Lord Milner, by the Boy Scout leader General Baden-Powell and by a number of daily newspapers. Warnings of a future German invasion were the theme of such novels as *The Riddle of the Sands* and such plays as *An Englishman's Home*: and there were writers who even thought that a struggle of race with race was natural and beneficial.

Little of this had registered with Baldwin or with most other people. It was a classical case of crying wolf. All that Baldwin could find to say on 4 August was: 'I think Germany has suddenly gone mad. I can't think of any other explanation that fits the case.' He seems not to have called in question the events leading to the catastrophe. But at least he did not suffer from the common belief that the war would be over in six weeks.

Baldwin was not among the more vociferous of his countrymen who, for a variety of reasons, were glad that war had come at last. His attitude, however, was quite unequivocal: every man must do his utmost for his country. He watched the first volunteers, splashed by mud from taxi-cabs, as they marched down Kensington Gore and 'I wished that I was with them. I wanted to do service for my country'. At forty-seven he was too old to join the services despite his early training with the artillery. At the same time he was still too junior in Parliament to have much say in the direction of the war. Before long his frustrations gave way to horror as the casualty lists came in. His cousin Kipling lost one son, Bonar Law lost two, and there were many others killed and maimed among the families of his friends. As the war dragged on, the casualty lists loomed ever larger in his mind and came to dominate his thoughts to the very end of his political career. Under the shadow of another war, he said in 1936: 'If the dead could come back to life today, there would be no war. They would never let the younger generation taste what they did . . . we are still finding and burying the bodies of those who fell twenty years ago.'

These young deaths aggravated his middle-aged frustration. He felt, as did Law, that it did not matter what happened at home to the older men provided they did everything in their power and strength to help their country in any capacity to which they might be called. He was not called to do anything. His wife could at least throw herself into work for the Red Cross, Belgian refugees, hospital duties and packing parcels for the troops, and his daughters followed her lead. Oliver, his elder son, joined the army in 1917. Baldwin was overcome with a sense of his uselessness: it was almost an affront to his virility. All he had was his considerable wealth, and he assuaged his vexation by dipping into his pocket. He paid the Friendly Societies contributions of every serviceman in the West Worcestershire constituency, as his father had done during the Boer War, contributed to war charities and to hospitals; in all he paid out something like £40,000. He sold iron and steel shares to raise £50,000 to buy War Loan. Nor did his private charity cease. He had an overdraft of £60,000 by 1917 and the family's style of living declined.

One or two minor Parliamentary jobs came his way. He worked long hours and filled two notebooks as a member of the committee which reviewed the cases of enemy aliens who had been interned. He sat on two other committees, one dealing with War Office contracts, one with post-war trade problems. This work did not satisfy him and he plunged momentarily into despair. He would be more use doing local work in Worcestershire, he told his wife; 'I am no good here, better go back'. She replied: 'Let's give it ten years,' that is in the Commons, and so he hung on. Mrs Baldwin subtitled a photograph of her husband on a tennis-court with the words: 'He also serves who only stands and waits.'

He was unhappy, too, like others, about the inefficiency and slack conduct of the war, and he was one of a 'ginger' group who rose in the Commons to ask awkward questions about army purchasing, billeting, and the supply of munitions. He rejoiced when Prime Minister Asquith formed the first Coalition Government in May 1915, bringing in such Conservatives as Curzon, Law and Chamberlain. When Lloyd George became Secretary of State for War, he was less certain, suspecting that his real aim was the premiership. Baldwin and seventy other Conservatives determined to block his way and they had semi-conspiratorial meetings at Baldwin's house in Eaton Square. Mrs Baldwin observed their comings and goings, some of them furtive and some excited, and promptly dubbed it the 'gunpowder plot'. Eventually, however, even Baldwin had to admit that Prime Minister Asquith had lost his grip; defeat followed defeat and the casualties were appalling. Reluctantly, he concluded that a change in leadership was overdue.

He talked it over with his cousin, Rudyard Kipling, and 'was highly pleased to find that he had come to the same conclusion about the Government that I had, and by the same road, after almost as long and anxious a cogitation. We have common puritan blood and he said a thing I have so often said and acted on: "When you have two courses open to you and you thoroughly dislike one of them, that is the one you must choose, for it is sure to be the right one." How much happier not to be made like that!' The deed was done in December 1916, when Lloyd George became Prime Minister with Law as his second-in-command, Chancellor of the Exchequer and Leader of the House. Baldwin had never trusted Lloyd George, so it was ironical that his arrival as the leader of a new coalition led directly to the end of Baldwin's long frustration.

Law was looking around for a Parliamentary Private Secretary with no one particular in mind. He sought advice from various people and it was Ralph Blumenfeld, editor of the *Daily Express*, who suggested Baldwin. Law, of course, knew him and had known his father; one was an iron merchant, the other an ironmaster, though they came from very different backgrounds, Law being a Glaswegian-Canadian. He had, however, been long enough in the House of Commons to know how gentlemen arranged such things. He invited Baldwin to play tennis with him at his house in Kensington and, as they relaxed after the game, casually enquired whether Baldwin would like to be his PPS, immediately adding that he did not 'suppose I should care for it'. He would also be required, Law nonchalantly remarked, to answer for the new Financial Secretary, Hardman Lever, who had no seat in the Commons and was shortly to be despatched to Washington.

Baldwin was delighted and within a few months was confirmed as Joint Financial Secretary to the Treasury, an onerous job since he had to reply in the Commons to all points of detail concerning the massive wartime estimates. 'It is all exceedingly exciting,' he wrote to his mother, and then, swanking a bit, added: 'One is in the very centre of the spider's web and as I always wanted a full-time job, I can't complain now I have got one . . . I never sought a place, never expected it and suddenly a way opened.' Was it not the hand of God? One man did not think so. Beaverbrook thought that Baldwin's promotion came because 'he was rich enough to entertain among Members of Parliament and win friends for himself and his chief'. Even more cynically, Wickham Steed of *The Times* suggested that Baldwin's appointment 'was made on the assumption that he was discreet enough to be "safe" and "stupid" enough not to intrigue'.

Soon Baldwin was answering questions as if to the manner born. Set debates he found trying because, as he said, he started well and then 'got muddled and talked nonsense'. The work was arduous both in and out of the Chamber. Three mornings a week he was at the Bank of England battling with the choleric governor, Lord Cunliffe. Occasionally he deputized for Law as Leader of the House, responsible for arranging the daily business. He was delighted to overhear, as he passed through the Lobby, a Member say of him: 'That's the hardest worked man in the House of Commons.' Of course, Baldwin commented, it wasn't true, 'but I preened myself and did the goose-step to the smoking-room'. Nevertheless he began to feel that strain which was to haunt him throughout his official career: 'I get quite stupid by Sunday,' he wrote, and then he took himself off for long, healing walks on the Sussex Downs. But he would not grumble: 'If I had been younger I should have been in France and probably underground by now.'

He became a popular, trusted figure in the upper reaches of the Government, and some delicate tasks were assigned to him. An awkward situation had arisen when Beaverbrook, as Minister of Information, was accused of wasteful spending and of mixing private business with public service. It was really Law's job to defend him but because of his well-known intimacy with Beaverbrook he felt he could not properly do so, and Baldwin had to do it for him. It was not easy because MPs on both sides of the House distrusted the whole concept of propaganda and feared that this new bogey might be carried on into peacetime. Baldwin took the accusations point by point, revealing their inaccuracy and drawing out much of their sting. The Ministry, he promised, would disappear with the end of the war. Meantime it was essential in dispelling ignorance of Britain's vast war effort and also to counteract the German propaganda which sought to split the Allies: 'Unless people have faith in their Allies and have faith in the cause, it is impossible for them to hold together to the end.' Beaverbrook had taken on a most difficult and thankless task, and all that Baldwin asked was 'give him a fair chance and judge him by results . . . Do not let us allow the personality of an individual to warp our judgement as to the value of the work he is doing or the means he employs in doing it.' What he said was well received but it was probably Tim Healy, Beaverbrook's Irish friend, who really saved the day by managing to sidetrack the issue into the bogs of Irish politics.

A favourite theme of Baldwin was the need that would arise for extreme economy after the immense spending of the war years and the dangerous inflation of prices. The House was duly amused when he added that after the war the Government of the day must choose 'its most repellent personality and make him Chancellor of the Exchequer'. Baldwin's occasional humorous sally endeared him even to Prime Minister Lloyd George, with whom he was never on real terms of intimacy. Baldwin referred to him at this time as 'that strange little genius who presides over us', and often met him at the political breakfasts Lord Derby gave during the war. On the day Lloyd George was to score a parliamentary victory in replying to Maj.-Gen. Sir Frederick Maurice's charge of making inaccurate statements on military matters, Baldwin buttonholed him: 'You know, P.M., that for ten years we have been trying to catch you deviating by an inch from the strict path of veracity. We never succeeded. But now others think they have got you and they will find out this afternoon that they have caught you speaking the truth. They will have the shock of their lives.' Lloyd George roared with laughter and afterwards told the Cabinet that he had 'been caught telling the truth'.

Most people, Baldwin among them, felt that the war would never end, and in September 1918 Northcliffe, the British propaganda chief, lugubriously observed: 'None of us will live to see the end of the war.' Two months later, quite suddenly, the exhausted war machines rumbled to a confused halt. An armistice was signed on 11 November 1918. The streets of London and the great cities filled up with revellers, and even the troops in France, stunned by the sudden silence of the guns, held parties in bistros and messes and told each other 'roll on my demob'. In many thousands of British homes there was mourning for those who could never be demobilized from the foreign earth in which they lay. Baldwin's mood was more in tune with that of the mourners than of the revellers. In the Lobby that afternoon the old Labour MP William Crooks took Baldwin's hand and said tremulously: 'This is a great day.' Baldwin replied: 'Yes, but I feel like crying myself.' Crooks told him: 'I have had my cry this morning.' Baldwin went to a short thanksgiving at St Margaret's: 'My brain is reeling at it all. I find three impressions strongest: thankfulness that the slaughter is stopped, the thought of the millions of dead and the vision of Europe in ruins. And now the work! Pick up the bits.'

The Coalition leaders agreed that, as the House was eight years old, it was time for a General Election. This took place in December 1918. The registers were incomplete, the electorate apathetic. Lloyd George and the other men who had 'won the war' were returned in an overwhelming Coalition victory of 516 seats.' Many MPs were new to the Commons and Baldwin did not care for the look of some of them. Maynard Keynes overheard him refer to them as 'hard-faced men who looked as if they had done well out of the war'. So, indeed, had Baldwin himself, a principle shareholder in Baldwins Ltd, which is perhaps why his ever-restless conscience now led him to make a grand yet practical, certainly unparalleled gesture. With elaborate secrecy he addressed a letter to *The Times* over the initials 'F.S.T.' His letter read in part:

Sir, – It is now a truism to say that in August, 1914, the nation was face to face with the greatest crisis in her history. She was saved by the free-will offerings of her people. The best of her men rushed to the colours; the best of her women left their homes to spend and be spent; the best of her older men worked as they had never worked before, to a common end . . .

Today, on the eve of peace, we are faced with another crisis, less obvious, but none the less searching. The whole country is exhausted. By a natural reaction, not unlike that which led to the excesses of the Restoration after the reign of the Puritans, all classes are in danger of being submerged by a wave of extravagance and materialism. It is so easy to live on borrowed money; so difficult to realize that you are doing so.

It is so easy to play; so hard to learn that you cannot play for long without work. A fool's paradise is only the ante-room to a fool's hell. How can the nation be made to understand the gravity of the financial situation; that love of country is better than love of money?

This can only be done by example, and the wealthy classes have today an opportunity of service which can never recur.

They know the danger of the present debt; they know the weight of it in years to come. They know the practical difficulties of a universal statutory capital levy. Let them impose upon themselves, each as he is able, a voluntary levy. It should be possible to pay to the Exchequer within twelve months such a sum as would save the taxpayer fifty millions a year . . .

I hoped that someone else might lead the way. I have made as accurate an estimate as I am able of the value of my own estate and have arrived at a total of about £580,000. I have decided to realize 20 per cent of that amount or, say, £120,000, which will purchase £150,000 of the new War Loan, and present it to the Government for cancellation.

I give this portion of my estate as a thank-offering in the firm conviction that never again shall we have such a chance of giving our country that form of help which is so vital at the present time.

The bonds were duly cancelled, in fact they were burned under the eye of the appropriate Minister, no less than the Financial Secretary to the Treasury, Baldwin himself, who afterwards said he very nearly stepped forward at the last minute to stop a fifth of his fortune going up in smoke. Few followed his lead. He had hoped for a subscription of £1000 million but only a bare half a million came in. Even the anonymity was shortly stripped from the man Baldwin referred to as Ferdinando Smike-Thomson.

Baldwin, Joint Financial Secretary during the latter part of the war, battled on in that office after the war, serving altogether almost four years from the age of fifty to fifty-five. He did not want to stay in the job for ever, for by now his political ambition had been whetted, but at this time he saw no hope of advancement. He stood in the shadow of the great eminences of the Coalition, Lloyd George at the height of his power, Austen Chamberlain, Churchill, Law, Birkenhead, Horne: such men were not to be easily displaced.

While Baldwin quietly cultivated his garden at the Treasury, his seniors strutted and fretted their hours upon the brightly lit stage in Paris and Versailles. It was they who negotiated the peace treaties and who joined in founding the League of Nations. It was only with the consequences of their acts that Baldwin would have to cope, a fact of which happily he was unaware. Of course he had his private opinions. While welcoming the Covenant of the League of Nations, he was perfectly aware that the absence of the United States from its own creation – vetoed by the Senate – meant that the British Empire, if it came to the push, would probably have to support the burden of sanctions single-handed; aware, too, that the peace treaties, so ill constructed, almost ensured that, in Lord Esher's words, 'a future war on a bigger scale becomes inevitable'. His cousin Kipling showed him a letter from the former President, Theodore Roosevelt, alluding to the League as an idea of those who 'want everyone to float to heaven on a sloppy sea of universal mush'. Baldwin would discover the truth of this in later years; meantime his own judicious view was that the League faced two obstacles, 'the prejudice of people who think it can do nothing and the support of people who think it can do everything'.

Baldwin was made a Privy Councillor in May 1920, a sign that he was regarded as a permanency on the political scene. Thus encouraged, he pressed forward rock-solid in that turbulent House of Commons, an inoffensive, business-like man untouched by the vogue for violent language of such as Churchill, who referred to Bolshevism as 'foul baboonery', or the Prime Minister himself, still 'fighting Prussianism' but now discovering it among the workers.

Baldwin had come to be on close terms, both politically and socially, with the sad and lonely Law, the Conservative leader in the Coalition, as close, he thought, as anyone except Beaverbrook. Then in May 1920 he had a shock: 'Bonar took my breath away the other day by saying to me: "Would you like to go to South Africa?" To which I said: "No, I don't think so. In what capacity?" "To succeed Buxton." [i.e. as High Commissioner and Governor-General] "Are you joking?" quoth I. "No," said he, "Well," said I, " there are plenty of men who would do that job as well or better than I: I think I am more use at home." "Would you like Australia?" said he. "Not a bit," said I. "Well", quoth he, "I thought you wouldn't look at it!" ' Baldwin chose to regard this offer as a compliment but to his mother he wrote of 'this slippery world of Government. And I can tell you it's a curious world'. He added: 'You can rely on me carrying on Father's tradition.'

Why did Law seek to divert Baldwin into what amounted to political exile: was it a stratagem whispered by Beaverbrook, jealous of Baldwin's friendship with Law? Was it part of some cat's-cradle plot of Lloyd George? Law's conduct is the more inexplicable since, when he was about to resign office on health grounds, he successfully pressed Lloyd George to offer Baldwin the post of President of the Board of Trade with a seat in the Cabinet. Baldwin accepted, though lamenting Law's departure to the point of telling him that, when he heard he was retiring (though not, as it turned out, for ever), 'I nearly took advantage of the shuffle to go back to private life and to business'. Yes, a very 'curious world'.

The morning the new Cabinet Minister walked into his office at the Board of Trade, the miners went on strike, the owners declared a lock-out, a state of emergency was declared and troops were moved into the coalfield. It was April Fool's day, 1921. Happily, Baldwin was not required to deal with the matter; since a general strike was feared, Lloyd George himself took over; and Baldwin, remaining silent in Cabinet, watched his manoeuvres with attention, little knowing how personally he himself was to be involved with the miners only a few years later. Eventually union solidarity cracked and 'the red revolution was postponed once more', as Tom Jones, Deputy Secretary of the Cabinet, put it. But only 'postponed', not settled, as Baldwin knew.

'The business of a Minister is different from that of Financial Secretary,' Baldwin informed his mother in May 1922. 'I have less work in the House except when I have a Bill.' Now he had *the* controversial Bill of the Session', and went off to prepare his speech in the country cottage he rented at Vann, in Surrey. The Bill, which he had inherited, was for the Safeguarding of Industries by putting duties on certain 'key' imports; it was controversial because safeguarding was a would-be bromide word for 'protection', but the Free Trading Liberals, in and out of the Cabinet, were not deceived.

For Baldwin the going was rough. The Bill, he explained, would stimulate home production and thus reduce the number of unemployed, then hovering around the two million mark. He conceded that it was not the complete answer to all Britain's economic problems and he ventured upon a brief discourse on the facts of economic life. British exporting, upon which the country depended, was made more difficult by high tariffs prevailing abroad. The European exchanges had broken down as a result of post-war financial chaos and until they were restored prosperity would be delayed. But he thought that Britain could make up for what she had lost by going after something fresh, by, for example, intensifying the development of the Empire and pushing into the markets of the East and of South America. Britain's staple industries – coal, iron and steel – were languishing. There were however signs of a recovery in the United States and that often led to a boom in the world at large. He ended with the words that were to be repeated down the years by successive British Governments: 'Every deliberate stoppage of production in this country is a deliberate lowering of the standard of life for our people.' The prospects of improvement in the social conditions of the British people were 'illimitable', but it could be brought about only by all Britons coming together: 'We should always remember what we have passed through in these last few years and, eager to serve the living, let us progress together with confidence in our future.'

The Bill itself did not pass easily. Baldwin on one occasion had to tell the Cabinet that if it would not agree to a certain duty he was ready to go. He won his point. Some of the Free Trade Liberals in the Commons demanded his resignation, but as one paper, *John Bull*, wrote: 'Mr Stanley Baldwin is not leaving the Board of Trade, much as the Prime Minister and the Coalition Liberals dislike his handling of the Safeguarding of Industries Act. What worries them is that Mr Baldwin is an honest politician.' The Bill received the Royal Assent in August, but was it not remarkable, his economist friend W. A. S. Hewins asked him, 'that a Government formed to prevent the adoption of a tariff should not only end by doing so, but should actually use a drastic closure and the Parliament Act [which exempted money Bills from the Lords' veto] to bring it about?'

Baldwin liked his job, and much enjoyed the audiences with King George v which he had as a Cabinet Minister. On one such occasion the King said to him, 'I could tell you the most extraordinary things that have been said if I chose,' to which Baldwin replied, 'I hope, Sir, that you will not write autobiographical articles in the press.' The King rejoined: 'Not till I'm broke!' But there were certain matters which worried Baldwin. Lloyd George dictated to his Cabinet as though he were still a wartime overlord and, Baldwin afterwards wrote, 'Ministers are not servants of the Prime Minister, they are responsible Cabinet Ministers'. His dictatorship could, Baldwin feared, lead only to the one-party State. He had shattered his own party, the Liberals, and if he continued as Coalition leader would eventually shatter the Tory Party as well. As Baldwin saw from the vantage point of a seat in the Cabinet, the Prime Minister's policies were makeshift and often, as far as industry was concerned, non-existent. He no longer cared for social reform; his foreign policies seemed unscrupulously aimed only at his own greater glory.

Then again, Lloyd George carried with him an odour of corruption. He had sought to corrupt the civil service, the judiciary and the newspapers. The Prime Minister's blatant sexual promiscuity was known to an increasing number of people, which was one of the reasons he was nicknamed the 'Goat'. Unfortunately the Prime Minister's lack of principle was infectious, and to illustrate this Baldwin invented an 'Afghanistan' proverb which found its way into the *Morning Post*: 'He who lives in the bosom of the goat spends his remaining years plucking out the fleas.' He was, Baldwin thought, 'a real corrupter of public life', and he remembered, too, that Law had once said to him that if he spoke for five minutes Lloyd George would have to retire from public life for ever. Baldwin was not afraid, even in the Cabinet, to stand up to Lloyd George on matters which concerned him as a Minister. Lloyd George once incautiously asked him for his opinion of a proposed Budget 'adjustment' and Baldwin replied that it made him feel 'as if he were a director of a fraudulent company engaged in cooking the balance sheet'. The 'adjustment' was omitted.

Then came the 'Honours scandal', which occasioned debates in both Houses. Lloyd George had not started the system of giving honours to those who paid large sums to party funds; in the past those who were to receive honours had been vetted, if that is the right word, by the Chief Government Whip. Even this minor check had gone by the board and the matter came to a head in June 1922 when peerages were offered to three businessmen of dubious reputation, one of whom had been guilty of trading with the enemy during the war. Hastily Lloyd George conceded a Royal Commission to consider future procedure.

The Coalition showed signs of disintegrating and there were murmurs from the constituencies. The junior Conservative Ministers demanded a meeting with Austen Chamberlain, who had succeeded Law as leader of the Conservatives. Chamberlain told them that such a meeting was unprecedented and irregular but that 'his colleagues had decided that they might condescend to hear us'. The junior Ministers emphasized the importance of preserving the solidarity of the Conservative Party and of having a leader of their own who, though perhaps allied with some of the Liberals, would be more independent of Lloyd George. They were bitterly attacked by Birkenhead, who stated flatly that the Conservative Party's only hope was to stick to the Coalition. Their complaints, Birkenhead arrogantly told them, were stupid and disloyal. Baldwin remained silent at this meeting, from which the junior Ministers retired in anger, but it was obvious that the leading lights of the Cabinet in which he served were going to stick together come what might.

It was the end of the Session and Baldwin was feeling very tired; his doctor ordered a rest. Baldwin told a friend that he had been tired for two or three months; it was, he supposed, age. With mock whimsy he reported on the furrows in his cheeks, 'made by the salt tears of weary impotence in which condition are his body and what kind friends in old days for want of a better word used to call his mind'. He went off first to Worcestershire and reflected that 'country folk are my own folk: in London I am a stranger, in the country at home . . . I say to myself as I roll along with waistcoat open and bare-headed: "And this is the — fool that walked every morning along Buckingham Palace Road in a black coat." '

Worcestershire was not far enough away from London for Baldwin to be free of his ministerial cares nor of his nagging doubts about the Government in which he served. So at the beginning of September he and his wife were motored across France to a summer retreat they had found at Aix-les-Bains, the little spa in the Savoy mountains near the Lac du Bourget. There he ceased to read the newspapers; even official dispatches were sifted by Mrs Baldwin and only the most important were passed to him. While his wife took the cure, he walked and walked through woods and fragrant alpine meadows, 'up, up and ever up. Chestnuts, walnuts, acacias, vines . . . The lake has all the colours of Italy, varying its shades of blue from pale turquoise to aquamarine, while away to the south there stands the line of Alps with their everlasting snows catching and reflecting all the lights of heaven. My walks are a daily joy and I am rapidly getting into some sort of condition.'

As he climbed, far away from Cabinets and the intrigues which had sickened him, he turned over in his mind the way he had seen 'one decent fellow after another go to pieces' under the influence of the Lloyd George group. The morality, he felt, had been 'sucked out of them', and he feared that the same thing might happen to him. 'I want a cleaner atmosphere,' he wrote to a friend. 'Cowardice. Does the pig make the sty or t'other way on?' He recalled that Eric Geddes, a former Coalition Minister, had said to him, how 'we had lost all sense of proportion, and I did things of which I am now thoroughly ashamed'.

On the evening of 29 September 1922, a telegram summoned Baldwin to return home for a Cabinet meeting. 'I have been expecting it,' he told his wife. 'There is some devilment afoot and I must get back to back up poor dear old Austen.' Travelling overnight he reached London on the morning of 1 October. The immediate trouble concerned the likelihood of a war against Turkey; the real trouble was the Coalition Government itself, from which, walking amid the sunny hills of the Savoy, Baldwin had made up his mind to cut loose even if it meant withdrawing from public life altogether. Ambition, yes, but not at any price.

3
PRIME MINISTER, TEMPORARY
1922–1924

BALDWIN brought himself up to date with the newspapers on his journey back to London and observed mildly: 'We seem to have messed up everything in the Near East, from the year preceding the war till today.' By the time he joined the Cabinet meeting on the morning of 1 October 1922, the nature of the mess was all too clear to him. Turkey, who had been Germany's wartime ally, was still in parts occupied by Allied forces and in Constantinople the Sultan was under their thumb. But the Turkish Revolutionary Army, led by Mustafa Kemal, had swept the Greeks out of Smyrna and the Anatolian hinterland with much bloodshed and rapine and was advancing on Constantinople. This army paused outside the barbed-wire fortifications of Chanak, in the neutral zone guarded by the Allies, on 24 September. The French and Italians hurriedly withdrew their detachments, leaving the British under the overall command of General Harrington to face Kemal's troops alone.

In London the Big Three of the Government, Lloyd George, Birkenhead and Churchill, without consulting the Foreign Secretary, Curzon, ordered Harrington to inform the local Turkish commander at Chanak that unless he withdrew his troops, at a time to be decided by Harrington, British naval, military and air forces would open fire. 'The time limit should be short,' Harrington was instructed. Harrington negotiated with the Turks but they would not give way. The Government wired him to start fighting when he thought fit.

Baldwin was stunned: ultimatum! War! And so soon after the end of the war to end all wars, a war moreover to be waged by

Britain on her own, since the Dominions, except New Zealand, refused their support. In Cabinet Baldwin spoke up for the slighted Curzon, locked in 'battle single-handed against all the fire-eaters and warmongers'. But apart from the Minister of Agriculture they were alone. Lloyd George and Churchill were talking wildly of the 'battle for Christianity' and proposed to set the whole Balkans aflame in the cause. Baldwin soon realized that their rage for battle concealed an objective quite unconnected with defending the Allied post-war settlements. They had 'schemed to make this country go to war with Turkey so that they should have a "Christian" (save the mark!) war *v.* the Mohammedan and turn the Turk out of Europe. On the strength of that, they would call a General Election at once and go to the country which they calculated would return them to office for another period of years.' The sheer immorality of it took Baldwin's breath away.

His personal crisis was approaching fast and he drew strength for what he knew he must do from a letter which Law, the ex-Tory leader and still an MP, had printed in *The Times* on 7 October. England, Law wrote, could not alone 'act as the policeman of the world. The financial and social condition of this country makes that impossible'. The Straits were not especially a British interest. Moreover, the British Empire, which included the largest body of Mohammedans in any State, ought not to show 'any hostility or unfairness to the Turks'.

Baldwin was summoned to a meeting of the Conservative members of the Cabinet on 10 October – the date Harrington had set for the expiry of his ultimatum to the Turks. Austen Chamberlain, the Tory leader, proposed that the Tories in the Cabinet should go to the country under the Lloyd George banner as a Coalition, that it should be done as quickly as possible without any consultation with the party and before the party conference in November. This was Baldwin's moment: 'I arose and spoke and told them that I for one could not and would not do it. I must be free and stand as a Conservative; I could not serve under Lloyd George again. The rest of the Unionist Ministers were aghast . . . They will follow the G. (Goat) and I can't so it means that I shall drop out of politics altogether . . . I shall never get a job again.' Chamberlain's proposal won the day. At the request of Law and Amery Baldwin did not immediately resign, but the Government realized that he, the quiet little President of the Board of Trade, was a challenge to all those whom Beaverbrook called 'the glittering birds of paradise' on the Front Bench.

Baldwin, however, was not quite alone in Parliament; Sir Leslie Wilson, the Tory Chief Whip, was with him, so were the right-wing Tories, Asquithean Liberals and of course Labour. Was it, Baldwin wondered, just possible that a great slide away from the Coalition had begun? But even if it had, he was too junior to turn the slide into an avalanche. Law alone could do that and Baldwin asked him directly 'if he would come out and lead the party'. He meant, of course, lead the party out of the Coalition and hence bring down the Government. Law was disinclined, uncertain of sufficient support, knowing that it would mean unpleasantness with many with whom he had worked during and after the war; and he was a tired man with no ambition left. Baldwin continued to press him. If you don't come out, Baldwin told Law, 'you are leaving all the white men on the beach. They can't get on without you to lead and it means we shall all just sink out of politics and leave them to those people who are not so honest'.

The build-up against the Coalition began in earnest, and among those pleading with Law to sound the tocsin were some Under-Secretaries, back-benchers led by Samuel Hoare, Lord Beaver-brook, the Fourth Marquis of Salisbury and such diehards as the Duke of Northumberland, Page Croft and Joynson-Hicks. Not all of them were entirely disinterested: Bridgeman noted in his diary that 'the more aspiring of my colleagues are on Bonar's doorstep looking for high office'.

By this time, Chanak, the immediate cause of the political unrest, had faded from the picture. Just seventy-five minutes before the zero hour fixed for 10 October, the Turkish general had agreed not to attack. But the tide continued to flow strongly against the Coalition, and the issue now was its political survival. Austen Chamberlain, rigidly loyal to the Coalition, determined to flush out the malcontents: as he wrote to Birkenhead, 'they must either follow our advice or do without us, in which case they must find their own Chief and form a Government at once. They would be in a damned fix!' He called a meeting of all Conservative MPs for Thursday 19 October at 11 am in the Carlton Club.

The lobbying intensified. Baldwin stated categorically at a meeting of dissenting Under-Secretaries that whatever happened, nothing would induce him ever again to serve under Lloyd George, and he began recruiting other rebels. Some MPs were still luke-warm, hoping that Chamberlain might unbend a little. Most of them, however, would follow Law's lead, but would he lead, would he even attend the Carlton Club meeting? Only on the very eve did Law make up his mind. He would go to the meeting, but a question still remained – what would he say?

On the morning of the nineteenth Baldwin and his wife were driven to a side street, whence he went on foot to the Carlton Club, then situated at the corner of Pall Mall and Carlton Gardens. Despite a chill wind a crowd had collected, and Law drove up in Lord Derby's car to mild applause; Austen Chamberlain (elected leader in the same club eighteen months before) and Birkenhead were just as mildly booed. Inside, the anti-Coalition MPs were in a good mood: they had just heard that in the by-election at Newport (Monmouthshire) the Tory had been elected, beating the Labour candidate despite a Liberal running as well, which meant that the Coalition was unnecessary. It was therefore singularly insensitive of the prim, monocled Chamberlain, who was in the chair, to lecture the meeting on the necessity of a Coalition Government as the only alternative to Labour rule.

Baldwin spoke next. What he had to say took him a bare eight minutes but his every word hit home. He supported the motion drafted by Hoare 'that the Conservative Party, whilst willing to co-operate with the Coalition Liberals, should fight the election as an independent party with its own leader and its own programme. . .' Baldwin, putting the views, as he said, of a minority in the Cabinet, asserted that the Conservatives in the Coalition government had made a 'fatal mistake' in agreeing to a General Election without asking the party whether its members wanted to continue the arrangement made in 1918. Then he turned on the Prime Minister himself. Yes, he said, Birkenhead was right when he called Lloyd George a dynamic force. He is, and that is the trouble. 'A dynamic force is a very terrible thing; it may crush you but it is not necessarily right.' That force, 'that remarkable personality' of Lloyd George, had smashed to pieces his own Liberal party; given time it would destroy the Tories too; 'the process must go on inevitably until the old Conservative Party is smashed to atoms'. Look what it had already done between himself (Baldwin) and Austen Chamberlain. They held the same views on the political problems of the day: they esteemed each other; they both sought to give service to the State: 'But the result of this dynamic force is that we stand here today, he prepared to go into the wilderness if he should be compelled to forsake the Prime Minister, and I prepared to go into the wilderness if I should be compelled to stay with him ... that process must go on throughout the party. It was for that reason I took the stand I did, and put forward the views I did. I do not know what the majority here or in the country may think about it. I said at the time what I thought was right, and I stick all through to what I believe to be right.'

Baldwin's fusillade was followed up by the big gun of Law, who said that he attached more importance to keeping the party united than to winning the next election, and therefore very reluctantly he would vote to end the Coalition. He sat down to excited cheering. The motion was carried by 185 votes to 88; the Tories were a party once more and the Coalition was over. Within three hours all Ministers had resigned, and the King sent for Law, who agreed to form a Government, subject to his election as party leader. In later years Baldwin rather than Law got the credit as 'Saviour of the Tory Party'. John Gunther wrote in *Inside Europe* (1936): 'One of the most obscure public men in England brought down its most celebrated figures through a largely moral and emotional appeal. The lumbering tortoise tripped the bright sharp fox.' Baldwin himself, a decade later, made it all sound much more premeditated than it had been: 'In those days', he told Tom Jones, 'I had developed a protective barrage of innocence in the midst of wickedness. I gradually covered myself with stripes in the jungle until I got into a position where I could hurl my pebble and bring him down.' At bottom the coup was not an affair of personalities. Tories in the constituencies were tired of the Coalition. To them Lloyd George had simply ceased to serve any essential purpose. Nor was there a plot in the sense Birkenhead meant when he talked of Tories being 'frightened by a few old diehard majors in the clubs'. Certainly Baldwin had no kinship with them. As he had already shown, he was much more in sympathy with such Tories as Edward Wood, George Lloyd and J. W. Hill, who wanted to avoid class conflict, to further working-class welfare and to stimulate a national solidarity through a modest and moderate Christianity.

How soon the elation of the Tory victory of 19 October evaporated! Gloom fell quickly upon the victors; the vanquished as speedily regained their spirits. Both were justified. Lloyd George, reported by Hankey, the Cabinet Secretary, to be in 'great form – absolutely hilarious', awaited with glee the errors he expected the new team would make, ensuring his own return to power. As Lloyd George supposed, Law found Cabinet-making uncongenial; he became yet more lugubrious, for he had little ambition to be Prime Minister. His choice of Ministers was restricted because, as Churchill said, he was confined to choosing a 'Second Eleven', the First having taken their bats home.

Baldwin obviously had to be given a job, and despite misgivings about his lack of experience, Law offered him the post of Chancellor of the Exchequer. Baldwin hesitated and suggested Reginald McKenna, a Liberal who disliked Lloyd George and had been a wartime Chancellor, but McKenna had no seat and preferred to continue as Chairman of the Midland Bank. Baldwin then accepted. Curzon, who had resigned from the Coalition just in time, remained the Foreign Secretary; Neville Chamberlain, Austen's half-brother, came in as Postmaster-General, it being believed that his name would buttress the administration. Others who received Cabinet office for the first time were Bridgeman (Home), Amery (First Lord, Admiralty), Wood (Education) and Lloyd-Greame (Board of Trade). A General Election was set for 15 November 1922.

Baldwin and Law thought an election, though not constitutionally necessary, was clearly desirable if only to allow the country to express its opinion on the change-over. An election manifesto was drafted by Amery, which, among other things, committed the party to make no fiscal changes before a second appeal to the nation: this pledge was to have significance in a year's time for Baldwin himself. For the rest the Government campaigned, in Law's words, on 'tranquillity and stability at home and abroad so that free scope should be given to the initiative and enterprise of our citizens, for it is in that way far more than by any action of the Government that we can hope to recover from the economic and social results of the war'. There would be an end to 'meddle and muddle'. There would be drastic economies in Government expenditure to reduce taxation, revive trade and bring down unemployment.

For the first time in his career Baldwin, as second man in the Government, had to campaign nation-wide. He did well; even the far from uncritical Beaverbrook wrote: 'He spoke with success. He said nothing sensational. He made no spectacular promises. He went before the electorate as a plain businessman representing a plain business Government out to do a solid job of work. And the electorate liked it.' Among Baldwin's personal pledges as Chancellor was to negotiate payment of the debt – 'to the last penny' – incurred with the United States during the war. (His implementation of this came near to losing him his job.) He also set the tone of the Government by stressing its 'modesty' as opposed to cleverness; this came naturally to Baldwin, who often lambasted the intelligentsia – 'a very ugly word for a very ugly thing, bearing the same relation to intelligence that the word "gent" does to gentleman'. Lord Robert Cecil, who was to be Privy Seal, put the same idea in different words: England, he said, preferred to be governed by second-class intellects rather than by second-class characters (though Law's Government actually contained three Fellows of All Souls).

For all that, when polling day arrived on 15 November the voters were confused. A variety of parties and half-parties sought their favours; Lloyd George Liberals, Asquithian Liberals, Coalition Tories, Tory Tories, the Labour party with its ragbag of attitudes and intentions, the I.L.P., the Communists. The politicians themselves were bemused. They had lost touch with the voters; they did not know what the public really wanted. In fact they did not exactly know who the electing public were. The Representation of the People Act (1918) gave the vote to women over thirty; it also increased male electors, who no longer needed to be house owners but could vote if they had a six-months residential qualification. Plural voting was abolished, except for graduates with university votes and those who owned business premises as well as dwelling-houses (these exceptions were removed in 1948). The electorate almost trebled, became an enigma to politicians so that, as Maurice Cowling puts it, they 'were trying not merely to say what electors wanted to hear but to make electors want them to say what they wanted to say in the first place . . .'

Somehow the Tory 'tranquillity' at home and abroad got through to them and appealed. They gave Conservatives 344 seats to Labour's 138, Asquithian Liberals 60 and Lloyd George Liberals 57. Baldwin, with a majority of 5,443 at Bewdley, said the victory was due to people believing Lloyd George's remark that Law was 'honest to the verge of simplicity'; according to Baldwin they

replied, 'By God, that is what we have been looking for,' and voted
Tory. Very few triumphant Conservatives knew or cared that in
numbers of votes cast they were in a minority. Labour for the
first time were the second largest party in the Commons, and they
elected the handsome orator Ramsay MacDonald to be chairman
and leader of the Parliamentary Labour Party. Some militant left-
wingers were elected, among them John Wheatley, Maxton, Shin-
well and Tom Johnston.

Baldwin, confirmed as Chancellor of the Exchequer, quickly got
down to business. Facing a likely budget deficit of £65m., he
demanded of his colleagues 'very considerable reductions of expenditure'. Then there was the pledge to settle the funding of
Britain's £978m. war debt to the United States. Baldwin with his
wife and daughters set sail on December 27, in the *Majestic*, for
New York; with him went his friend Montagu Norman, Governor
of the Bank of England, and his principal Private Secretary P. J.
Grigg. The seas were rough and most of his party were prostrate
with sea sickness; Baldwin was in tip-top form, even visiting the
engine-room at the height of a tremendous gale. Though he never
flew and became nervous in a motorcar, he was relaxed on board
ship.

The negotiations were complex. The British hope was to reduce
the onerous terms of repayment and to tackle a basic question:
should Britain have to pay her debts before receiving those owing
to her from her European Allies, particularly as much of her
borrowing from America had been channelled to those Allies?
France and Italy said they could not pay until they received
reparations from the erstwhile enemy and the Russians would not
pay because they had gone Communist. The Americans were
determined that Britain should pay; her entanglements with
Europe were just too bad. As for the fact that many of Britain's
debts were caused by her having to buy from America goods sold
at inflated prices (thus creating yet more US millionaires), that
also was just too bad. Nor would they lift their tariff barriers to
allow Britain to repay her debt in kind. 'Uncle Shylock' would
drive a hard bargain, just as he had in forcing Britain to abandon
her old alliance with Japan in 1921. Britain and America
thoroughly distrusted one another throughout the inter-war years,
and what pro-Americanism there was among Englishmen was
confined to public oratory. Nevertheless Baldwin and the Cabinet

did want to honour the country's debt because it was necessary to demonstrate that Britain's word was still her bond and because they did not want America to cut herself off from Europe.

Baldwin's talks were amicable. The debt had been contracted in the form of 5 per cent obligations payable on demand; in the meantime interest was accruing at about £50m. a year. But the best terms he could get was for Britian to pay 3 per cent interest for the first ten years and 3½ per cent for the remaining fifty-two years, i.e. an annuity of £33m. for ten years and one of £38m. for the next fifty-two years, thus stretching to 1984, a year to which Orwell had not yet given a sinister significance. It was much less than the Americans wanted, but too much for Law, who ordered Baldwin home for consultations. The terms had, however, already leaked to the press and been made to sound like an American 'take it or leave it' proposition; indeed Hughes, the U.S. Secretary of State, made it clear that if the 'offer' was not promptly accepted and the negotiations dragged on until the Presidential Elections, there would be no chance of American help in the financial reconstruction of Europe and in settling the reparations issue.

When Baldwin landed at Southampton on 29 January 1923, he went a long way to corroborate Birkenhead's witticism about him: 'The man has foot-and-mouth disease; every time he opens his mouth he puts his foot in it.' He told journalists, though believing his remarks to be 'off the record', that he was in favour of accepting the American offer – this before, as the King's Private Secretary tartly pointed out, it had been discussed, let alone approved, by the Cabinet. Baldwin followed this bloomer with another. Any settlement, he said, must needs satisfy the American Congress, which meant it would have to satisfy the mid-western States, most of whose Senators and Representatives came from agricultural communities and had no idea of international finance. Swift o'er the wire the electric message went: The British Chancellor of the Exchequer says that the average Senator is 'a hick from way back'. Baldwin was afterwards to say that he had rather that his tongue had been torn out than have talked to the press at Southampton.

Law raged furious, mainly because the impression had been given that the deal had already been concluded though, *pace* Law's biographer, it had not. 'I should be the most cursed Prime Minister that ever held office in England if I accepted those terms,' Law told Baldwin bluntly. Now Baldwin's career was in the balance. If the terms, to which he had given his public approval, were not accepted by the Cabinet, he would have to resign. If the terms *were* accepted by the Cabinet then Law would resign, and the Government would collapse.

Baldwin agreed at a Cabinet meeting on 30 January 1923 that the terms were harsh; he thought that the Americans, who had made immense fortunes before they entered the war, could have been more generous, but they worshipped the 'God Almighty dollar'. Nevertheless he stuck steadfastly to his view that the offer was the best that could be got and that it should be accepted. Law was vehement; he thought the debt should be repudiated altogether rather than burden the coming generation. He felt so strongly that, most unethically, he wrote an anonymous letter to *The Times* arguing his case. But the Cabinet, to his chagrin, was against him and for Baldwin, with only two exceptions. In that case, said Law angrily, 'if it were decided to accept it would have to be without him'. The meeting adjourned. But the next day, after Law had received a deputation from his colleagues, he yielded. Baldwin had won, and the agreement was signed. Whether the agreement was right or wrong was for long debated; at the time Baldwin was supported by the Treasury (except for Keynes), the City, banking and most men-in-the-street. Yet there was much to be said for Law's point of view: that the Anglo-American settlement should have been concluded only as part of a general settlement of inter-Allied debts and reparations, and that if it had been delayed better terms might have been obtained; or, as Keynes put it: 'It is the debtor who has the last word in these cases.' Indeed it is. In 1932, the Allies, having given up hope of further reparations from Germany, wiped the slate clean and put into effect a policy of coordinated default to America.

Baldwin's colleagues looked at him with new eyes. Here was a man who could override the Prime Minister and get away with it. This was not the action of a weak or timid man. Something more of the real Stanley Baldwin was revealed in his Commons speech defending his settlement, when he displayed the wider horizons of his thinking, his attitude of tolerance and peacefulness and idealism: 'It is no good trying to cure the world by spreading out oceans of bloodshed. It is no good trying to cure the world by repeating the pentasyllabic French derivative "Proletariat". The English language is in thought the richest in the world. The

English language is the richest in the world in monosyllables. Four words of one syllable each are the words which contain salvation for this country and for the whole world. They are "Faith, Hope, Love and Work". No Government in this country today which does not have faith in the people, hope in the future, love for its fellow men, and which will not work and work and work, will ever bring this country through into better days and better times, or will ever bring Europe through or the world through.' Were these not the words of a true leader of men, an embryonic Prime Minister?

Baldwin opened his first (and last) Budget on 16 April 1923. Financially the year had turned out surprisingly well; there was a £100m. surplus which was largely applied to debt redemption – that debt, he said, 'insistant and knocking at the door of this generation'. He announced a sinking fund to meet statutory repayments and, he hoped, to promote British credit. He expected a surplus in the next financial year and in anticipation took sixpence off standard income tax, then five shillings in the pound, and a penny off a pint of beer. Baldwin's speech, full of lively asides, was remarkably brief, one hour twenty minutes, by the standards of those and later times. The praise that pleased him most came from the Treasury official, Sir John ('banknote') Bradbury: 'Your effort goes far towards re-establishing that faith in human nature which was so gravely jeopardized by my Treasury experience!' [i.e. under the Lloyd George Coalition]. Baldwin's budget was, of course, condemned by left-wing Labourites not on specific points but because, as James Maxton of the I.L.P. frankly declared: 'My function as an agitator is to fan the flames of discontent.' The acidulated Philip Snowden, no Marxist, simply called it 'a rich man's Budget', but approval greatly outweighed criticism.

He took his success ruefully. 'I am going through that dangerous time', he wrote, 'when all men speak well of me. But it won't turn my head nor will it last.' While Baldwin's reputation blossomed, that of the Government as a whole decayed, and Law, according to Maurice Hankey, Secretary to the Cabinet, 'looks more than ever like a mute at a funeral or an undertaker's assistant'. Law, in fact was stricken with a fatal disease and resigned the premiership in May 1923. Who was to succeed him? Law placed the choice firmly in the King's hands, since an heir was far from apparent. Curzon was the most distinguished and by far the most experienced member of the cabinet; that he was a peer was not automatically exclusive. (Lord Halifax was considered as P.M. in 1940). Yet some of those who had worked with him thought that the idea of him as Prime Minister was grotesque: he was erratic, pontifical and outside (and sometimes inside) foreign affairs incapable of sound judgement. To imagine him hobnobbing with the TUC was impossible.

If not Curzon, then who? Could it possibly be the Chancellor of the Exchequer? Baldwin himself thought not. He had been only two years in the Cabinet, a mere seven months at the Exchequer, and felt 'genuinely frightened' at the idea. He was willing to serve under Curzon, anyone who could keep the party together (although whether Curzon could do so was doubtful). Certainly Baldwin would not put himself forward nor ask anyone else to do so; in fact during the decisive weekend of May 19-20 – it was Whitsuntide – he secluded himself at Chequers (which Law had given him the use of since he did not wish to use it himself) and played Patience in the Long Gallery. The King sought elsewhere the advice which Law refused to proffer, although Law did once say to an intimate that he supposed it would have to be Baldwin, rather in the spirit of the French critic who, asked to name France's greatest poet, replied: 'Victor Hugo, hélas.' Law had not forgotten his pique when Baldwin had carried the day in the Cabinet over the American war debt settlement. The King turned to Balfour, as the only living ex-Conservative Prime Minister, and nephew of the great Lord Salisbury. Balfour had no doubts: it must be Baldwin; he had, though he did not say so, suffered too long the vagaries of Curzon. The King's other adviser, Lord Salisbury, preferred Curzon, but there were few to agree, and so Balfour carried the day.

Baldwin was called to the King on 22 May 1923, and agreed to form a Government, the King hoping he would retain the angry Curzon and try to bring in the other ex-coalition Conservatives. The announcement of Baldwin's accession came as a shock to the public; only afterwards was it to seem inevitable. *The Times* wrote: 'Mr Baldwin's political career has been without exception the most amazing of modern times.' Baldwin at first could scarcely credit what had happened: 'I'm not a bit excited', he told his mother, 'and don't realize it in the least.' So short a time before, the great ones and the clever ones in the Coalition

Government had seemed immeasurably above him; now they had fallen from their perches and here he was, a person of 'the utmost insignificance' as Curzon had called him, in No. 10, surrounded by staff ready to do his bidding. He spoke later of the 'succession of curious chances' that had put him there; and indeed he would scarcely have become Prime Minister if Law had lived to bring back the 'birds of paradise'. With complete truth Baldwin could say: 'I never sought the office. I never planned out or schemed for my life.' But then he fell to pondering how many small things, scarcely noticed at the time, fell into place; humble as he was in his heart of hearts, imperfect as he knew himself, could not the hand of God be discerned once more working out a pattern imperceptible to mere mortals?

When reporters congratulated him as he went up the steps of No. 10, he replied: 'I need your prayers rather than your congratulations.' He meant it. Prayer was the focus of his life: 'Every morning when we rise', his wife once told a friend, 'we kneel together before God and commend our day to Him, praying that some good work may be done in it by us. It is not for ourselves that we are working, but for the country and God's sake. How else could we live?' Yet, if on the surface Baldwin showed few signs of emotion, Tom Jones noticed during an interview with him in the Cabinet room that 'his face started twitching, he rolled his tongue about and looked into space . . . ' His calmness was fragile; only the twitching escaped the iron self-control. It took Baldwin some time to realize that he was the most powerful man in Britain, and then he wrote to his Warwickshire friend Phyllis Broome: 'Here is the biggest job in the world, and if I fail, I shall share the fate of many a better man than I. But it's a fine thought, isn't it? And one may do something before one cracks up' – which several times in the next fourteen years he was to do.

Then he turned to focus more directly on what he thought the theme and style of his administration should be. Almost thinking aloud, he said in Edinburgh in July: 'I want to see in the next year or two the beginning of a better feeling of unity between all classes of our people. If there are those who want to fight the class war we will take up the challenge and we will beat them by the hardness of our heads and the largeness of our hearts. I want to leave this country, when my term ends, in better heart than it has been for years. I want to be a healer . . . '

But before he tackled the 'class war', he had the novel task of putting together a Cabinet. If possible, the King had hoped, it would include some of the ex-Coalition Tories, but Birkenhead made it known that he would not serve under Baldwin nor sit in the same Cabinet as Curzon (who agreed to remain as Foreign Secretary). Austen Chamberlain was approached, invited to Chequers – but only after all the ministerial positions had been filled. Baldwin was clumsy and Chamberlain lost his temper. Baldwin tentatively inquired only whether he might think of joining the Cabinet in a few months time; meanwhile what about the Washington embassy? At this disrespect for his political importance, Chamberlain flared up and Baldwin hurriedly back-pedalled. Chamberlain asked him why he had not consulted him when forming his Cabinet and Baldwin abjectly replied: 'I am very sorry. I never thought about it. I am very sorry.' Afterwards Chamberlain wrote to Birkenhead: 'I have been deeply wounded. I feel some contempt for Baldwin's weakness, which does not, however, remove my sense of his discourtesy and his blundering approaches to me . . . '

As a result, Chamberlain pointedly absented himself (as did Birkenhead) from the party meeting in the Hotel Cecil at which Baldwin was elected leader. His half-brother Neville, however, remained as Minister of Health and later became Chancellor of the Exchequer after various others had been approached: for the time being Baldwin took on the Exchequer as well as the premiership. Baldwin, bearing in mind hard heads and class war, appointed his friend J.C.C. Davidson, 'David' his *fidus Achates*, as Chancellor of the Duchy of Lancaster; under this 'cover' Davidson made ready for countering general strikes or other forms of civil disruption. Hankey was still Cabinet Secretary; he and Baldwin never hit it off and it was Hankey's deputy, Tom Jones, who became the intimate adviser and chronicler of the P.M.

Once Baldwin appointed a Minister, he never fussed him by interfering. 'He was extremely nice to his Ministers', wrote Davidson, 'but never showed the slightest inclination to come to decisions on their behalf.' That is why he often sat silent at Cabinet meetings, 'entering the arena only at the end of a discussion or when the Prime Minister's views were particularly needed. He wasn't – nor did he ever attempt to be – a Winston or a Lloyd George, but the chairman of a competent board of managers . . . ' He was always accessible to a Minister in trouble or doubtful about a decision as he was to heads of departments and civil servants: his door was always open. Whether a Minister benefited much from a private chat with him was sometimes debatable. Oliver Stanley, when Minister of Labour, sought his advice. Baldwin listened attentively for ten minutes, then said: 'Well, we've had a very interesting conversation, Oliver. Always remember you can come at any time to see me when you have a problem to discuss. Now go away and make your decision for yourself and I'll back you.' (Incidentally, Baldwin seems to have been the first Prime Minister to use Christian names habitually with his colleagues, though Lloyd George called Law 'Bonar' and Churchill 'Winston'.)

Baldwin spent long hours on the Front Bench – too long, thought those who were never quite sure whether he was thinking or woolgathering. In fact, he was often looking with curiosity at his neighbours, taking the 'feel' of the House. In the smoking-room he did not in the least mind being buttonholed. All the same he worked hard at his papers, at least at this period. Despite his appearance of nonchalance he felt the strain of making frequent speeches to large audiences outside Parliament. He admitted to drinking more champagne than he had ever done; it 'bucked him up', he found, for delivering a speech. He rather deprecated speech-making, telling one audience that he 'had never yet known a good workman who could talk nor a good talker who was a good workman'. In reality, he was an excellent speaker, not merely the national leader but the national bard, declared Arthur Bryant. His tone exactly fitted the mid-1920s mood of the country at large and when he took to broadcasting his style was as appropriate to the listener's sitting-room as a comfy armchair.

The famous BBC announcer Stuart Hibberd wrote in his autobiography *This – Is London* that

unlike other Prime Ministers Baldwin nearly always made a point of coming to the studio to broadcast, rather than speak from 10 Downing Street. His broadcasts were an object lesson. He had one or two little mannerisms, which probably resulted from his intense concentration on what he was saying, and I doubt if he was conscious of them. Apart from Hugh Walpole, Mr Baldwin was, as far as I can remember, the only person who ever spoke into the microphone without a manuscript, and, watching him in action, I am sure a manuscript would have

bothered and not helped him. He spoke somewhat slowly and deliberately, without using very much voice – a good point this, for a House
of Commons man – from a few headlines written on a piece of folded
paper, rather like a spill one uses to light a pipe; and this he kept
twisting and turning nervously around his fingers as he spoke. Now and
again, in searching his mind for the right word, he would momentarily
open and close his lips without any sound emerging, but generally his
thoughts flowed swiftly and his sentences were short, crisp and clear –
in fact, ideal for broadcasting purposes.

He kept his body quite still – unlike many other famous broadcasters –
made no gestures with his hands, and remained all the time looking
directly at the microphone, as though engaged in earnest conversation
with a man immediately opposite him in the room. As soon as he had
finished and the red light had gone out he would take his cherry-wood
pipe from his coat pocket and start filling it, ready to light up immediately he got outside the studio. While waiting for the engineer's report
on his broadcast he would laugh and joke like a schoolboy, and talk in
the most homely and natural way.

Tom Jones helped him with his speeches but did not write them.
Jones talked over the substance with him; then Baldwin rehearsed
the speech with him. If his speeches are to be criticized it can only
be on Francis Williams's grounds, that he seemed to feel that if a
thing had been well said, there was no need to do anything about it.

Baldwin needed always peace and relaxation. At No. 10 he did
not find them. To him it was a comfortless place. It had in 1923
only one bath (put in for Disraeli); the curtains dated from Mrs
Gladstone's time, had been repeatedly washed, had shrunk and
were too short for the windows. Chequers, however, delighted the
Baldwins, for it had been tastefully refurnished by its donors,
Lord and Lady Lee of Fareham. In its spacious acres Baldwin
could wander at ease wearing what he liked. What he liked was an
old lounge suit, shabby felt hat, baggy trousers and thick-soled
shoes. In this *tenue* he attended the Eton-Harrow match at Lords.
It was all too much for the *Tailor and Cutter*; in fact, declared
that arbiter elegantiarum, it was suburban. But the country as a
whole rather liked that; it was at any rate a change from the long-
maned Welsh spellbinder, Lloyd George, and his super-smart
Birkenhead.

Baldwin saw clearly that the primary aim of his Government
was to find jobs for some at least of the 1,300,000 male unemployed.
The way to do this was to stimulate the export trade, and to do

that it was essential to 'settle Europe. We can't wait for emigration and Empire development'. Much, therefore, depended on Curzon and Baldwin found, he 'is difficult, very bad-tempered in the forenoon but better as the day advances'. Settling Europe primarily meant settling France who, under the spiky Raymond Poincaré, was determined to screw the last mark of reparations from defeated Germany. To make sure of this France and Belgium had marched in and occupied the Ruhr on 11 January 1923 – 'like sticking a penknife into a watch', said Baldwin – and stimulated a separatist movement in the Rhineland. This made the Germans less able to pay reparations, and they began passive resistance. Curzon did his best; he pointed out that Britain and the United States were also owed reparations, and that Poincaré had no right to drive the common debtor into bankruptcy. By August 1923 the mark had fallen to 19,800,000 to the pound and was to fall yet further; inflation swept through Germany, and the Cuno Government resigned. Cuno was replaced by Stresemann and Communist uprisings were ruthlessly put down. Still Poincaré persisted. At this point Curzon, suffering from phlebitis, dropped the reins he had so sedulously kept out of the hands of his colleagues. Baldwin took them up.

Baldwin, holidaying at Aix, found that the Ruhr 'has a way of joining me last thing at night and being with me first thing in the morning'. But not the Ruhr alone. On 31 August 1923, Mussolini, the bombastic Italian dictator, attacked and occupied the Greek island of Corfu; this was in revenge for the murder of three Italians who, under the League's auspices, were reviewing the boundary line between Greece and Albania. Poincaré showed signs of supporting Italy in the hope of re-establishing an understanding with her. Greece appealed to the League and Baldwin ordered a strong line to be taken at Geneva in her support. Eventually, a settlement grossly unfair to Greece was made and the League's prestige was damaged, but at least sanctions and war had been avoided.

Baldwin began his talks with Poincaré in Paris on 19 September; it was the first and last time he consulted personally with a foreign head of state. His success was partial. Poincaré's adieu to Baldwin was a kiss on both cheeks, but the kiss was that of Judas, as Baldwin swiftly discovered. Poincaré had lied to him. Baldwin had understood that if Germany ceased passive resistance in the Ruhr, France would open negotiations. A few days later Stresemann, the

German Chancellor, ordered an end to the resistance in the Ruhr and cancelled the suspension of reparation deliveries. But the French continued to refuse negotiation and went on supporting separatist movements on the left bank of the Rhine. From this time dated Baldwin's distrust of the French.

But he wanted to avoid a breach since he knew that perhaps half the Cabinet and half the country were sympathetic to Poincaré's objective, which he revealed to a newspaper correspondent, of making sure that Germany could not raise her head for at least fifteen years. To that, many Britons would shout 'hear, hear', and some, who had read Keynes's *Economic Consequences of the Peace* (1919), would have welcomed a revision of the whole Versailles treaty. Still, Baldwin achieved something: he had got Poincaré to renounce publicly the territorial ambitions he was suspected of having in Germany; and had agreed to the Anglo-German idea of a committee to inquire into Germany's capacity to pay reparations and into stabilizing her currency and balancing her budget. An American, Gen. Charles G. Dawes, was to see fair play as chairman of the committee which in due course produced the Dawes plan.

At the height of the Ruhr crisis Baldwin indulged in what his biographers call a little sabre-rattling. The rôle sounds an unlikely one for him; yet defence did concern him even in this early post-war period when militarism was anathema, when the generals and admirals had become scapegoats and Lloyd George's 'Ten Year Rule', adopted by the Cabinet in 1919, prevailed: the rule said that the armed forces should plan their needs and strategies on the assumption that there would be no major war for ten years. The military machine was partly dismantled. During the Ruhr crisis it happened that the Salisbury-Balfour committee reported on the state of air defence and Baldwin put forward the Cabinet's conclusions. France was thought to have a first-line strike force of 600 planes. So Britain would add 34 squadrons to the 18 already existing as defence against 'attack from the strongest Air Force within striking distance' i.e. France's, and he added the memorable words: 'We must remember that our island story is told, and that with the advent of the aeroplane we shall cease to be an island. Whether we like it or not, we are indissolubly bound to Europe.' The latter thesis was not accepted by all Conservatives nor by all the military planners.

France was unlikely to attack Britain, though as Balfour said 'where national security is concerned, even the unthinkable must be faced'. If no action were taken, 'the impossible may after all occur. Even if it does not occur, the mere fear of it may, in quite conceivable circumstances, greatly weaken British diplomacy and may put temptation in the way of French statesmen which they would find hard to resist'. But to many, all and any war was unthinkable, and the Parliamentary Labour Party here began its long and inglorious opposition even to parity in arms let alone to superiority. Nor, in what was to be so brief a Government, did Baldwin's thinking stop there; it was he who created the Chiefs of Staff Committee distinct from the Committee of Imperial Defence. But he did not rescue the Army, whose very existence seemed indecent to many; neglected, it sank into torpor.

While Europe remained unsettled, industrial discontent increased at home, particularly among the miners, even though they had a low unemployment rate – 2.9 per cent compared with shipbuilding's massive 32 per cent. What happened was that, when the French occupied the Ruhr, German mines closed down and British coal exports went up, and so did profits. This encouraged the miners to demand a minimum wage agreement, which Baldwin would not support on the grounds that, as in 1921, it would be bad policy to give one section of industry such an advantage when other sections were suffering a depression. Moreover, the Ruhr situation was no more than temporary. German coal would be mined again and once more compete with that of Britain. Baldwin, who knew the chaotic, out-of-date state of the industry, planned its complete reorganization, but this was resisted by the coal owners.

An Imperial Economic Conference opened in October, at which the Dominions, particularly Canada, were bluntly assertive in their demands to be consulted before foreign policy decisions were taken in their name; and they wanted a preferential tariff. Baldwin, Curzon loftily observed, 'never opens his mouth and leaves the entire lead to me', adding: 'Nothing can exceed the cheerfulness, good temper and courtesy of Baldwin, except his impotence.'

That Baldwin was politically impotent was a view not generally shared. Winterton, a member of the Government though not in the Cabinet, thought that Baldwin had quickly established himself as 'no makeshift leader . . . the old type of English statesman, fair-minded, judicious and responsible'. Surprisingly, some Labour leaders agreed; more surprisingly still, one of them was the Socialist intellectual, Harold Laski. In the souls of such, Baldwin had earlier discerned 'a certain crystalline hardness'. But here was Laski wishing that Baldwin was in the Labour party: 'I rarely escape the conclusion, especially when I read your major speeches', he wrote to the Prime Minister, 'that it is tradition rather than fundamentals that has put you among the forces of the Right.' The Labour men liked him for his honesty and lack of bluster; and of course for such remarks as 'a man who made a million quick ought not to be in the Lords but in gaol' (said to have greatly shocked Law) and for the fact that Baldwin publicly and without dismay envisaged a time when Labour would sit on the Government benches. Baldwin was also at one with the Trades Union Congress leaders in seeking advance by negotiation rather than either by the sledge hammer of revolution ... or by the crafty and insidious scattering of sand in all the gearing wheels of industry. At the same time, Baldwin's precautions against revolution or sabotage continued under Davidson.

Soon Baldwin began to despair of finding an orthodox remedy for the continuing unemployment. Before the National Union Conference at Plymouth in October 1923, he told his friend Bridgeman that he feared their remedies for unemployment were mere temporary palliatives. Even if Europe recovered, competition with British commodities would increase because of cheap European labour and low exchange rates. Only thorough-going Protection could, he now concluded, save Britain, and it had to be introduced quickly, certainly before the winter of 1924–5. There was a snag. Law had won the 1922 election with a pledge that no fiscal change would take place without another appeal to the country. So, logically, a General Election was necessary. Bridgeman sought to dissuade Baldwin or at least to get him to delay until the electorate had been 'educated' on the subject. Instead Baldwin made one of his abrupt decisions, an impetuous leap in the dark. Soon after Parliament reassembled in November 1923, he informed the country that he was going to dissolve and call an election.

Tory MPs doubted Baldwin's sanity: why risk Law's splendid majority? Moreover, MPs 'have all paid one thousand pounds to get there in election expenses and their wives do not want them to pay another thousand with a risk of being thrown out'. The King remonstrated with Baldwin: Europe was in a turmoil; besides, he pointed out, Baldwin might lose. Curzon wrung his hands at the decision taken by what he called 'the arbitrary fiat of one weak and ignorant man'; Derby declared that Europe was ruled by madmen (Poincaré and Mussolini) and England by a damned idiot. Baldwin never quite knew how he got his reluctant Cabinet to agree: 'I came to the decision by myself,' he said long afterwards, 'and how I drove that Cabinet to take the plunge, I shall never know. I must have more push than people think.'

But *would* tariffs decrease unemployment? On this critical question, according to Hankey – admittedly a none too friendly witness – Baldwin consulted no one, even though there was a wealth of official information available in the Treasury, Board of Trade, Board of Customs and Inland Revenue. Lloyd-Greame, President of the Board of Trade, knew quite well, wrote Hankey, that the figures were against tariffs helping unemployment; when Neville Chamberlain, Chancellor of the Exchequer, instructed his secretaries to gather figures to support Protection, he 'found that they all told the wrong way!' Indeed, a year later Baldwin was running the country quite happily without his tariff mandate.

In fact Baldwin's devotion to fiscal change was not the only reason for his snap decision. He told Tom Jones that 'I had information that he [Lloyd George] was going protectionist and I had to get in quick, otherwise he would have got the party with Austen and F.E. and there would have been an end to the Tory party as we know it.' In short, he raised the Protection issue in part for party ends and to save the country from the pernicious influence of Lloyd George. His distaste for Lloyd George was particularly strong at this period, amounting almost to obsession, shared also by Mrs Baldwin, who at Astley before the election showed Tom Jones a photograph album in which 'I came across a picture of Lloyd George as Chancellor of the Exchequer defaced. How they do hate him!'

A tariff to Baldwin's mind had other advantages. It might win back the Chamberlain–Birkenhead ex-Coalitionists – and so it came about, and without causing the resignation of such Free Traders in his Cabinet as Salisbury, Devonshire and Derby. Baldwin went into the election on 6 December with the support of Chamberlain and Birkenhead and the chance of reuniting the party – if the Tories won. Baldwin had gained a point. But he may be thought to have lost one when, the day the election was announced, the Lloyd George Liberals reunited with the Asquithians under a temporary concordat and between them put up 453 Liberal candidates.

The Tory campaign was mishandled and muffled. The tariff proposals were imprecise and differently stressed by party speakers. As Austen Chamberlain wrote: 'The impression left on everyone's mind is of doubt and perplexity ... We have had six columns of speeches from the P.M. in less than a week and no one knows what he means.' It was Balfour and his Protectionist equivocations all over again. The Tory party organization, short of money, was a none too willing participant: 'a gamble which gives most of the cards to the other side,' said Admiral Reginald Hall, then head of the organization. All the same, Central Office's 'toothcombing' of the constituencies convinced them that the Tories were sure of a majority of thirty over Labour plus Liberals.

They were wrong. Election day, 6 December 1923, was as foggy as Conservative policies, and the results were 'disaster', a 'landslide', said Derby. The Conservatives lost over ninety seats and Liberals won where Conservatives had sat for forty years; Labour gained new seats in industrial areas. The figures were: Conservatives 258, Liberal 159, Labour 191. Baldwin, whose own majority was only slightly increased, returned from Worcestershire to No. 10 the day after the poll. In the Cabinet Room, wrote Jones,

there were no Ministers about to welcome him, only a couple of private secretaries and the usual messengers. It was all very depressing. He took out his pipe and tried to put a cheerful face on the situation. We ordered tea and I was then left alone with him. We went through the staggering results recorded in the afternoon papers. He scanned eagerly the fate of men personally known to him ... I tried to comfort him with the thought that he had fought an honourable fight, free from exaggeration and abuse. He referred to Mrs Baldwin's disappointment, 'after having just settled in here. We must go and live in a small flat. Our town house is too expensive for us.' Then his talk took an ethical turn: 'Everyone who tries in politics to do the things he believes in simply and honestly is sure to come a smeller. The martyrs did. Christ did.' The expression was new to me and I suppose is the equivalent of the colloquial 'cropper'. I wanted very much to ask the P.M. how he came to make the initial error which has led to this debacle, but I felt it would be too cruel.

The election result brought the thunder, the lightning and the hail on Baldwin's head. Even in the Cabinet there were mutterings that Baldwin must go. Derby, the great Lancashire potentate and War Minister, wrote: 'It saddens me to think that the Prime Minister should, within six months of taking office, bring us to this . . . It looks as if the Conservative Party has been smashed up for all time.' Curzon talked of 'the incredible folly of our leader'. As for the Protectionist policy Baldwin had forced on his party, it was totally discredited. Plots proliferated, short-lived though they were, to replace him as leader by Austen Chamberlain or Derby, for some of the ex-Coalitionists now thought they saw the way to crush the man who had helped destroy them. Or at least, would not Baldwin seek an arrangement to keep the Socialists out by combining with the Liberals? No, he would not. Davidson was probably echoing his master's voice exactly when he wrote 'any dishonest combination of that sort – which means the sacrificing of principles by both Liberals and Tory to deprive Labour of their constitutional rights – is the first step down the road to revolution'.

When Parliament met on 15 January 1924, a hostile amendment on the address was carried by seventy-two votes, all but eleven of the Liberals joining with Labour to defeat the Tories. Baldwin's Government resigned next day. Four days later, he left Downing Street, remarking to his wife in front of the staff: 'I'm glad we are leaving these lodgings Cissy, the beds are damp.' 'But, Stan, dear,' she protested, 'they're our *own* beds.'

Baldwin was at first far from downhearted. Indeed, at his last Cabinet, Curzon noted — no doubt with some mortification – that the Prime Minister 'seemed quite cheerful today and unconscious of the terrible doom he has brought upon our party'. As Baldwin prepared his speech just before his defeat in the Commons, Jones found him almost merry: 'I have not felt so well for a long time and I shall be tempted to be very vulgar in my speech,' he said. He wasn't, though he did write with unwonted venom about newspapers using on him 'a syphilitic dagger'.

His euphoria passed; he spoke to his friends of his 'mental debility being indescribable', of his need for rest and relaxation from those who sought him out for 'fourteen hours a day'. He had private worries too. His elder son Oliver, a neurasthenic victim of a hard war, was arrogant and offensive to his parents and mocked all they and his other relations stood for. His father's generation, he claimed, had betrayed his own. Oliver belonged to a Marxist group and spoke for Labour candidates during the election campaign. Baldwin's financial position, too, was shaky. He had £50,000 a year in 1914; now, out of office, his income was his dividend from Baldwins – and none had been paid for three years. He missed the Prime Minister's £6,000 a year. He had borrowed from his mother for his election expenses. He could, of course, realize capital; but instead in 1925 he sold his house in Eaton Square (to become the Belgian Embassy) – and still continued his generosity to those close to him who were in distress.

Few of his worries and debilities were visible to strangers. Dining at Trinity, Cambridge, in February 1924, he was introduced to A. C. Benson, Master of Magdalene, who recorded in his diary: 'I saw a plain pale little man by the Master whose face seemed familiar – a lifted eyebrow, a little smile, a perky curl of the lip . . . He struck me as a very good-natured, sensible, able, tired man but with plenty of stuff left in him, entirely unembittered and healthily detached.'

Plenty of 'stuff' indeed! Once the dust had settled, he looked on his handiwork and was not entirely displeased. He was glad that Labour had found its way to the Government benches; it was part of his 'healing' process; it also dished the Liberals, and Lloyd George, for ever as it turned out. He might also have agreed with the more calculating Neville Chamberlain that Labour was dished too: 'too weak to do much harm, but not too weak to get discredited'. He was right. After a bare year in office, they quickly vanished into the Opposition.

Baldwin did not fear that the Labour Prime Minister, J. Ramsay MacDonald, would irrevocably ruin the country. He was no roaring red. Baldwin rather liked him with his 'ravishingly musical voice, every syllable ringing of Utopia' (in A. J. P. Taylor's phrase), and believed he would act constitutionally and adopt a determined opposition to Communism and to direct action, which sought to gain power not from the electorate but by fomenting strikes. He agreed with MacDonald on 'fair play' on foreign policy, in return for which throughout 1924 Baldwin received a selection of Foreign Office papers and telegrams (except with regard to Russia) which ensured a continuity of policy. 'We are not going to fight the Labour Party with abuse,' he said in a public speech. 'It has to be fought by the only way that will ever win in this country, by substituting something better in the minds of the people. With us, no less than with the Labour Party, there is a desire to help the people of this country, to give them a better life and opportunities of education and self-betterment.'

Gradually Baldwin reasserted his authority in the Commons until it was he and MacDonald who stood out pre-eminent, with Lloyd George submerged. Yet Baldwin was, as he said himself, 'not a good leader of Opposition' – at least in the Commons – because, like Balfour, he could see all too clearly both sides of any question. Off the floor of the Commons, he was an excellent leader. The leading Tory ex-Coalitionists had been brought back from their sniping posts into the fortress and thought happily of the Ministries they would get on the Tories' return to power – an event which, after calm consideration, many thought would not be long delayed. So, wrote Neville Chamberlain, 'reunion has come at last'. It was, he thought, thanks to him.

The party's general tariff policy was quietly dropped. The electorate had rejected it, well and good: that was the end of it. It did not worry Baldwin. Jovially he told a meeting on 7 February 1924 of the Shadow Cabinet – which he was the first to institute with a secretariat, as he had instituted the back-bench 1922 Committee – that all that bothered him was that, at the party meeting when his leadership was to be endorsed, 'I shall have to do some skilful tightrope walking for which my figure is not well suited.' Well might Neville Chamberlain confide to his diary that Baldwin 'is not so simple as he makes out'. Baldwin himself told an audience at Stourport in 1925: 'If I pretended, as I may have done in the course of my career, that I was more simple than I really am, then you would know exactly how far I was deviating from the strict letter of the truth.'

Baldwin turned his attentions to getting ready for the next election. The Central Office had to be reorganized. Admiral Hall was replaced as Chief Agent by Sir Herbert Blain, general manager of London's public transport system, who proved an effective new broom. Not, however, for some years did finance become adequate. Baldwin also insisted that the constituencies should choose working-class candidates; otherwise 'if you are going to fight a party that has the choice of the whole population, you will never beat them in this world and, more than that, you will never deserve to beat them'. Directly at Baldwin's instigation a Policy Secretariat was formed as an adjunct to the Shadow Cabinet; it was headed by Col. L. Storr, under whom were such young men as Geoffrey

Lloyd and Robert Boothby. Outside experts were brought in to advise and all these were responsible directly to Baldwin.

Soon they were writing manifestoes; in pamphlets and otherwise, Hoare, Wood and Neville Chamberlain floated new ideas. But before starting his campaign Baldwin waited for the Liberals, brought together for the last election, to split up again; this they did on 22 April when Lloyd George condemned his leader, Asquith, for cooperating with Labour. In May and June 1924 Baldwin made ten major speeches during a tour of the country. In them he was careful to avoid any suggestion that the Conservative Party was the instrument of the rich against the poor. Resistance to Socialism as a doctrine, yes; but the aim must be to show that Socialism, being impractical, was not in the best interests of the working classes. Resistance for its own sake to *all* working-class demands was not his aim. Change there must be; Baldwin would have agreed with Burke that change 'is the most powerful law of nature and the means perhaps of its conservation. All that we can do and that human wisdom can do is to provide that the change shall proceed by insensible degrees.'

Baldwin's policy was amelioration, the relief of unemployment – the most important and difficult problem – the improvement of insurances, pensions and housing and other measures of social reform to be carried out with common sense and practicality. His colleagues, he told audiences, were going to produce long-term schemes to bring these about. There would be safeguarding of industry and Imperial preference was important; he deplored the Labour Government's repeal of the McKenna duties. As for defence and foreign affairs, Baldwin quietly criticized the Government's decision to postpone the construction of the base at Singapore, essential to Empire defence; he was prepared to accept limitation of arms so long as Imperial defence was not weakened. He made no excessive promises. To the Conservative Ladies of Essex he was frank: 'No Government can bring to the people all that they desire – very often they do not know clearly what they desire. But they want things to be different and they call on fresh Governments in the hope of getting it.' His campaign was hailed as 'the new Conservatism'.

The stolid-looking, pipe-smoking Baldwin had a surprising love of indiscretion, for what he was later to call 'appalling frankness'. Out he would come with startling revelations which, though often embarrassing to his colleagues, endeared him to the public. What *would* this chap say next? Even when he rambled among the platitudes, his audiences had to listen for fear of missing a bit of spice. Baldwin gave an interview to Wilson, a reporter on the right-wing *People* Sunday newspaper, in May 1924. First he offered yet another reason why he had called an election six months before. If the Tories had not gone to the country 'we should have died of dry rot in two years and Labour would have come in with a sweeping majority'. Then, under Wilson's expert leading, Baldwin burst out: 'I know I am abused and jeered at and intrigued against. But why?' It was, he said, because 'I was determined that never again should the sinister and cynical combination of the chief three of the Coalition – Mr Lloyd George, Mr Churchill and Lord Birkenhead – come together again . . . Before the election last year, I welcomed Mr Austen Chamberlain back, and I accepted his friends, though I could easily have stopped their return to our councils. With Austen came Lord Birkenhead, who attached himself to the strings of Austen's apron the year before very cleverly . . . But I am under no illusions as to Lord Birkenhead. If his health does not give way he will be a liability to the party. But can a leader in opposition shut the door to an ex-Minister?' (This sly reference was to Birkenhead's drinking habits.)

Devastatingly the indiscretions tumbled out. The Press Lords, Beaverbrook and Rothermere: 'They are men I would not have in my house. I do not respect them.' Beaverbrook: 'He had contracted a curious friendship with Bonar and had got his finger into the pie where it had no business to be. He got hold of much information, which he used in ways in which it was not intended. When I came in, that stopped. I know I could get his support if I were to send for him and talk things over with him. But I prefer not. That sort of thing does not appeal to me.' He did not spare what he called 'this Churchill plotting' – 'bad for the party, for all the young men who are looking to Toryism for the salvation of the country'. The intriguers simply wanted to go back 'to the old dirty kind of politics. Not while I'm leader of the party'. At this point, Wilson noted, 'Mr Baldwin yawned with disgust and weariness at discussing for so long so unpleasing a subject'.

When the article appeared, the Central Office were appalled and repudiated some parts of the interview, though admitting the accuracy of others: it did not specify which were true and which were not. It declared that the reflections attributed to him on well-known public men did not represent views he held. But, said the

Glasgow Weekly Herald, the personal passages were precisely those an interviewer would have found most difficult to imagine or invent. Privately, Tom Jones noted in his diary: 'Anyone who knows S.B. intimately cannot but feel that the interview reflects substantially his general attitude to politics and his colleagues.' The *Morning Post* observed that 'we are glad these things have been written in public, even if they have not been said'. Chuckling with delight, Lloyd George informed one of his meetings that 'Mr Baldwin is an honest man. He tells the truth, even in interviews.'

With the public the interview did nothing but good: honest Baldwin, the man we can trust because he tells the truth even about his colleagues! But it mortified some of his colleagues. Loftily, Austen Chamberlain observed to his sister: 'Baldwin does not interest or attract me. He seems to be stupid and incommunicative, and his habit of bursting out with some inconceivable folly . . . is both disconcerting and exasperating.' In a subsequent letter (14 July 1924) he thought that: 'No one seems to have much confidence in Baldwin except himself, but he seems to be thoroughly satisfied with what he does. It must at least be admitted that he takes his position seriously and works very hard!'

Baldwin could have tumbled the Labour administration at almost any time since it was propped up only by Liberal votes and made no effort to placate Liberal sensibilities. But he was loath to bring it down before it could be seen to have had a fair run for its money. After all, it had not imposed the threatened Capital Levy; it had not nationalized the pits and the railways; it had not 'socialized' anything. But then in August 1924 the Government, egged on by its left wing and by the I.L.P. Members of Parliament, went too far. It announced an agreement with Soviet Russia; there was to be a commercial treaty between the two countries with a most favoured nation clause and diplomatic status for the Russian trade delegation; and in another treaty the British Government would underwrite a loan to Russia, once the British financial claims dating from before the Revolution had been settled. Conservatives and Liberals alike condemned the terms. Baldwin would have accepted some form of commercial treaty but a Government loan and diplomatic recognition of an administration which had held on to power only by murder and torture was too much. MacDonald wanted the treaties to be ratified by Parliament, and this neither the Liberals nor the Conservatives would consider.

Meantime Sir Patrick Hastings, the Attorney-General, had

started a prosecution against a Communist journalist, J. R. Campbell, for incitement to mutiny. In the Communist *Workers' Weekly* he appealed to the armed services never to fire on 'fellow-workers' either in a class or military war. Some copies of the paper had been tossed into Aldershot barracks. The I.L.P. intervened and MacDonald ordered Hastings to withdraw the prosecution. The Opposition stigmatized this as political interference with the course of justice. MacDonald publicly denied being implicated or even consulted; later he said that he had been told of it but had not intervened. Both were lies. A sinister connection was suspected between the dropping of the prosecution of the Communist and the projected Anglo-Soviet treaties. Asquith, the Liberal leader, called for a Select Committee of Enquiry, which MacDonald could not accept because he feared that such an enquiry would reveal his prevarication. He could not refuse a Conservative censure debate, though Baldwin emphasized that his objection was to the proposed treaties with Soviet Russia rather than to the Campbell affair.

But then Baldwin decided that after all he would support the Liberal proposal for a Select Committee. This was effectively the end for MacDonald. It was better to be defeated at once than to be revealed as the Prime Minister who had lied to the House: further it was better to be defeated on the Campbell issue than on the proposed treaties with the Soviet. So he made the Government's handling of the Campbell case a vote of confidence and shortly after 11.00 p.m. on 8 October 1924 the first Labour Government was defeated by 364 votes to 198. MacDonald sought a dissolution and a General Election was fixed for 29 October. Never in his fifty years experience, commented Asquith, had he known of a Government which 'so wantonly and unnecessarily committed suicide'. Perhaps he was unaware of MacDonald's fears of exposure; so was Baldwin until, back in office, he called for the Cabinet records.

Baldwin campaigned on the Labour Government's failure to deal with unemployment, thus making the dole a 'hideous necessity' and running the risk thereby of habituating sections of the population to idleness and to believe that what they got from the State 'was an inalienable right'. He emphasized, too, that 'in a time of crisis the policy of the Labour Government is not decided by the Government but by those extremist forces that appear to control it'. Until MacDonald could rid himself of that Old Man of the Sea, the party he led 'would never be fit to govern. We cannot afford the luxury of academic socialists or revolutionary agitation.' Baldwin never impugned MacDonald's political character; he merely deplored his weakness, hoping that he would learn to resist the Left.

The fear of Bolshevist influence was widely felt and not without some cause: 'I think', said Baldwin, 'it's time somebody said to Russia, "Hands off England".' Scarcely had he uttered the words when the newspapers published the sensational 'Zinoviev' letter under headlines referring to a Soviet plot against Britain. The letter, signed by Zinoviev, Chairman of the Third International, and its British member, Arthur MacManus, was addressed to the British Communist Party, and urged its adherents to stir up the 'army of unemployed', to create Communist cells among soldiers, sailors and munition workers and to organize risings in Ireland and the Colonies. It warned the working class to distrust the bourgeois Labour Party. The letter's contents should have been true because they expounded the real policy of the Third International and Ramsay MacDonald himself amended and made stronger a Foreign Office note which was sent to Rakovsky, the Russian *chargé d'affaires* in London. The note peremptorily told the Russians that Great Britain would not tolerate such interference in her domestic affairs. When, however, a raging Labour Party (and Rakovsky) claimed that the Zinoviev letter was a forgery perpetrated by a Tory newspaper, MacDonald feebly claimed that he had not signed the amended draft of the note in his own hand. That the letter was a forgery has always been maintained by the left and its supporters but recent evidence adduced by Miss Sibyl Crowe, an Oxford historian (see *Journal of Contemporary History*, vol 10, no 3, July 1975), gives reason to believe that, as Baldwin always believed, the letter was genuine. The letter's effect on the outcome of the election was probably small.

Labour lost, yet Labour votes *increased* from 4.3m. to 5.5m., though they won only 152 seats. The Conservatives also increased their vote from 5.4m. to 7.4m. and won 415 seats, a resounding absolute majority of over 200. The real sufferers were the Liberals, reduced to 41 seats; even their leader, Asquith, was rejected in favour of an I.L.P. candidate at Paisley, and he shortly accepted an earldom. The Liberal Party, to Baldwin's satisfaction, had ceased to be a credible alternative governing party. Baldwin said: 'The next step must be the elimination of the Communists by Labour. Then we shall have two parties, the party of the Right and the party of the Left.'

4

PRIME MINISTER,
CONFIRMED
1925–1929

BALDWIN, the 'mediocrity' who had thrown Law's majority away, came back to No. 10 Downing Street confirmed in his office by a hefty majority. At fifty-seven, he was, Austen Chamberlain noted, a good deal changed and stiffened by his electoral victory – perfectly courteous, but not inclined to accept advice or suggestions, particularly about his Cabinet-making. He wanted to bring back the leading Tory ex-Coalitionists, but would they accept the authority of the man they had bitterly berated for his part in their downfall two years before? Baldwin was warned about them the day after the final election results were in. Col. John Gretton, chairman of Bass and an MP, wrote to him on 1 November 1924: 'I am sure the Coalition idea is not yet dead and the "Brains" still hanker after a Centre Party. I am sure that intrigues to displace you or, in the alternative, to smother you by a group of disloyal Ministers, will be made and at least the "Brains" will be greedy. But they really have counted for very little in the result of the elections. We have won our own cause and our principles and because the electors believe that you are a steady man and can be trusted . . . '

Baldwin knew this but appointed the 'Brains' nevertheless. He made Austen Chamberlain Foreign Secretary because, now that the Ruhr had been settled, he wanted a new start in relations with France, and Chamberlain was said to love France 'like a woman'. Curzon was displaced – 'a terrible slur on my administration,' he wrote – because his old acrimonies with France hung around him like a tattered cloak; he was given the Lord Presidency, Leadership

63

of the Lords and chairmanship of the Committee of Imperial Defence, but he, in whom Baldwin saw 'a vein of purist gold', died three months later. Another 'bird of paradise' brought back into the gilded cage was the brilliant and erratic Lord Birkenhead, for whom, as the interview in the *People* showed, Baldwin did not care; he was given the India Office, and soon after loftily remarked in a letter to a friend: 'It is of course a tragedy that so great an army should have so uninspiring a Commander-in-Chief. But this cannot be helped; and I think he will be well under control.' A copy of the letter was promptly sent to Baldwin by the eccentric millionairess Lady Houston. Both Baldwin and Birkenhead would change their minds about each other.

The most startling of Baldwin's appointments was that of Winston Churchill as Chancellor of the Exchequer. 'It was better', Baldwin told the King, 'to give him office now rather than run the chance of his having a grievance and being disgruntled at being omitted.' Or, as Austen Chamberlain said: 'If you leave him out, he will be leading a Tory rump in six months time.' He was not Baldwin's first choice for the Exchequer; he had again offered it to Neville Chamberlain, who, however, preferred to carry out the reforms planned in opposition, and took the Ministry of Health, which at that time carried out the functions of what became the Ministry of Housing and Local Government.

The choice of Churchill seemed precipitate but was not. 'The Treasury officials in the old days used to tell me that they believed Winston would make a good Chancellor,' Baldwin told Tom Jones. Moreover he would be better fully occupied with finance than in some office where he would be in danger of getting at loggerheads with Labour. Davidson thought the appointment 'genius'. 'You have hamstrung him, so that his hairy heels are paralysed.' Only Amery, appointed to the Colonial Office, feared that Baldwin's 'rash importation of Churchill into the key position in the Cabinet had, in effect, converted his Government into just that kind of Whig coalition which I had hoped the Tory Party had escaped by breaking away from Lloyd George in 1922'. But that was the point – Baldwin wanted to deprive Lloyd George for ever of his potentially most powerful ally for re-forming the old Coalition.

Baldwin's team was strong but he kept it on a light rein. As Eustace Percy, his President of the Board of Education, was to write: 'It would almost be true to say that he trusted his colleagues for all executive action and himself only for expounding their policies to the country in terms which public opinion would understand and approve.' Yet, though he sometimes sat silent in Cabinet, he was in command, 'always quietly but definitely in control', wrote Cunliffe-Lister, his Trade Minister.

He still sat constantly in the Commons, of which he was Leader, sensing its mood and atmosphere with the ear almost of a musician; but he felt strong enough now not to be its slave. He was dining alone one evening at the Travellers' Club when an agitated young man appeared: 'My Minister has sent me to tell you that we've just been defeated.' 'Very bad management,' said Baldwin, returning to his book. The young man insisted that they were expecting him at the House. Very deliberately Baldwin put down his knife and fork: 'Are you suggesting that I should interrupt my dinner and go round to the House just because a lot of middle-aged men behave like a pack of schoolchildren? We'll put down a motion and take the business again – preferably in Private Members' time.'

Baldwin was never very attentive to what the Conservatives from the constituencies had to say. Their National Union of Conservative Associations passed resolutions which he ignored; they called him 'one of the slowest-acting men in existence'; they said 'our loyalty is the same as ever, but it has got to be "On Stanley, On" '. He continually exasperated them; yet as a man and a leader he was much loved.

Soon after the election he announced the broad aim of his Government to an audience in Stourport: 'There is only one thing which I feel is worth giving one's whole strength to, and that is the binding together of all classes of our people in an effort to make life in this country better in every sense of the word. That is the main end and object of my life in politics.' As earnest of his intention, in March 1925 he refused to support a Conservative Private Member's Bill seeking to change the operation of the trade union levy paid by the unions to the Labour Party. Previously, union members who did not wish to pay the levy had to contract out, thus drawing attention to their anti-Labour views; the Conservative member Frederick MacQuisten wanted trade unionists to be obliged to contract *in*, that is, each union member should decide whether he wished to pay money to the Labour Party rather than having his contribution taken automatically unless he objected.

Most Conservatives fully approved the proposed change; but,

to their chagrin, Baldwin said 'no'. He insisted to his Ministers 'that one of the main principles of the Government's policy is to do everything possible to promote peace in the industrial world'. Such a measure as MacQuisten proposed was right, but must inevitably arouse acute controversy and embitter relations among those who alone were in a position to bring about the desired pacification. Somehow he made his colleagues take the point – it was not easy, but he did it, and Birkenhead passed a pencilled note across the table to him: 'I think your action shows enormous courage and for that reason will succeed.'

His speech in the House epitomized Baldwinism. He ended with these words:

For two years past, in the face of great difficulties ... I have striven to consolidate and to breathe a living force into my great party ... I want my party today to make a gesture to the country [of peace] and to say to them: 'We have our majority; we believe in the justice of the Bill which has been brought in today, but we are going to withdraw our hand, and we are not going to push our political advantage home at a time like this.' Suspicion which has prevented stability in Europe is the one poison which is preventing stability at home, and we offer the country today this. We, at any rate, are not going to fire the first shot. We stand for peace. We stand for the removal of suspicion in the country. We want to create an atmosphere, a new atmosphere in a new Parliament for a new age, in which people can come together ... I know – I am as confident as I can be of anything – that that will be the feeling of all those who sit behind me, and that they will accept the amendment which I have put down in the spirit in which I have moved it. And I have equal confidence in my fellow-countrymen throughout the whole of Great Britain. Although I know that there are those who work for different ends from most of us in this House, yet there are many in all ranks and all parties who will re-echo my prayer. *'Give peace in our time, O Lord.'*

Baldwin's amendment triumphantly won the day. Even the once 'wild' Clydeside Labour MP David Kirkwood thought that 'the word has become flesh ... that the antagonism, the bitterness, the class rivalry were unworthy and that understanding and amity were possible'. Baldwin's speech, that evening of 6 March 1925, reinforced the trade unions' belief in his essential honesty, however they disliked some of his policies. The deepest effect was on his Cabinet colleagues. None any longer thought him an outsider; he had shot up in stature, was robed with prestige and authority. From that evening he was seen as the natural Prime Minister, head and shoulders above the colleagues who once despised him, the master of his Government.

The MacQuisten affair was only one example of the Baldwin Government's beneficent intentions. In this, the glad confident morning of its days, it truly wanted to help all the people. Before long Neville Chamberlain, who believed that 'unless we leave our mark as social reformers the country will take it out of us hereafter', unwrapped a great packet of reforms, reforms within the nation's means, their extent tied only to trade and prosperity. Chamberlain would work out the necessary Bills – he submitted no less than twenty-five to his colleagues in November 1924 – and Churchill would find the money. His proposals were interlinked. Poor Law had to be changed before a Health Service could be properly organized; the development of National Health Insurance required the creation of a single health authority in each area. Again, if Poor Law was to be reformed the machinery of valuation and rating must be revised, as also the financial relations between the State and local authorities. To Chamberlain and Baldwin, it seemed just and decent that there should be proper pensions for widows and the elderly and that unemployment insurance should be augmented.

Before the end of the 1924–9 Parliament many of these projects reached the statute book, not always untrimmed by financial exigencies, and not always without creating anomalies. Over some matters the Cabinet bickered and Baldwin had to bestir himself. 'At first', wrote Bridgeman, 'he was disinclined to give a lead . . . though he got much better in throwing his weight at the right moment. I think his fault is to be too sanguine that things will come right without his having to take a strong line.'

Baldwin gave Chamberlain particular support for his plans to replace old slum property, after visiting slums in Glasgow and Dundee under the guidance of Medical Officers of Health. 'Oddly enough', he wrote to Davidson, 'I have never been in real slum houses and I, as near as two pins, sat down and howled: the whole thing came to me with such force. Five or six in one room. Think of the children!'

Baldwin himself drove through Cabinet and Parliament the formation of the Central Electricity Generating Board, financed half by Government stock, half by local undertakings. Since the C.E.G.B. was a monopoly it irritated Conservatives; since it was centralization, not nationalization, Labour opposed it as 'administrative and economic Bedlam'. But its effects were wholly admirable. By 1939 electricity output had quadrupled, its costs fallen, and it revolutionized alike industry and home. This was, then, what 'rationalization' – the vogue word of the 1920s – could do, and it was applied, not without struggle, to cotton (Lancashire Cotton Corporation, 1929) and to steel when Vickers, Vickers-Armstrong and Cammell Laird became the English Steel Corporation and uneconomic works were ruthlessly closed down. Rationalization, however, added to the already 1,250,000 unemployed, and retraining and resettlement schemes were started; new light engineering and chemical industries were established, but their development would take time.

Baldwin worried over the unemployed. He still felt a general tariff was the answer but election pledges precluded it. That was one of the reasons he backed the return to the gold standard which Churchill carried out in spring 1925. He believed it would revive trade, thus creating employment; and all but a handful of pundits agreed with him. The gold standard was seen as a means of restoring normality to the international trading monetary systems, whose dislocation by the war had led to galloping inflation on the Continent and the collapse of the central European currencies.

In essence it was a device for keeping the various national currencies at a fixed relative value. Imbalances in trading accounts between nations were supposed to lead to gold movements which automatically set in motion corrective forces designed to adjust relative prices and incomes to the required level and thus regulate the volume of home activity. It did not, and many years later Churchill said it was 'the biggest blunder' of his life. Its actual result was to overvalue sterling and send up the prices of exports. To counter this, industrial costs had to fall but most industrialists sought to do this by cutting wages, not by reorganizing. The gold standard also caused a money shortage at a time when plentiful credit was needed to develop new industries. Bank interest was kept high and that also discouraged enterprise. The City had to fund itself largely from the short-term deposits attracted from abroad by high interest rates.

What neither Churchill nor Baldwin would face was the unpalatable fact that the war had so damaged Britain – large portions of her assets had had to be sold – that she could no longer finance international growth on the pre-1914 scale. Britain was trying to play a fat Falstaff with insufficient padding. True, the encouragement of imports brought down the price of primary products and food; and the employed worker grew modestly prosperous, but, in a sense, at the expense of a bedraggled hungry horde of workless.

The gold standard in reality meant Free Trade. It was also deflationary, and it implied, as before 1914, the balancing of the budget. Thus, public cheeseparing was the order of the day and Churchill went to it with gusto. He balanced his budgets and produced surpluses – or did he? Davidson thought that 'Winston's budgets were in fact deficit budgets balanced by odd feats of arithmetic and other manipulations. It is not really the solid buttressed finance that we would expect. He did some very, very clever things and some very expedient things but expediency was not principle.' As Tom Jones observed: 'Winston is really gambling on the chance of a steady revival of trade in the next twelve months.'

Baldwin, as was his wont with Ministers, left the balancing (or faking) of the budget to his Chancellor. He was to suffer a rude awakening. Churchill, pursuing economies with all the single-mindedness that he had once pursued the Germans and would have liked to pursue the Russians, wielded his scythe on the Armed Forces. They were the biggest spending departments; they must make the biggest savings. In this he reflected the *zeitgeist*. Throughout the 1920s, writes Michael Howard, was to be heard 'the heavy and ominous breathing of a parsimonious and pacific electorate to the variations in which the ears of British statesmen were increasingly attuned'. In 1920 the Coalition Government slashed Armed Forces expenditure from £604m. to £292m. and over the next two years to £111m., around which figure it stayed until 1935.

None heard the heavy breathing more clearly than Churchill, 'who having spent five years at the Admiralty building up the Royal Navy was now spending another five at the Treasury trying with equal zest to cut it down again'. Nor was it only the Navy. He promised in 1925 a progressive £10m. annual cut in all Service estimates; that is, £31m. off in 1926–7 and £49m. off in 1927–8. He tried to halt the building of the Singapore defence system until Baldwin stopped him; he cut back the fifty-two squadrons scheme, thus stifling the aircraft industry. But his most dangerous clash was with the Admiralty.

Here he put Baldwin on the spot. Churchill argued that to accept the naval armament programme would mean the end of all Baldwin's cherished ideas of social reform. 'We should come up to the election with these enormous Navy estimates and nothing else to show. We should be accused of starting up the armament race all over the world and setting the pace towards a new vast war. I cannot conceive any course more certain to result in a Socialist victory.' The Navy was preparing for a war with Japan; there would be no such war 'in our lifetime', quoth Churchill. The battle between Admiralty and Treasury raged and it was a battle for Baldwin's mind – and the future of his Government, for resignations, including that of the whole Board of Admiralty, threatened.

Baldwin, as usual, temporized; there would be a Cabinet committee to investigate the future programme of naval construction. But the affair widened; now it was a split between the Old Coalitionists (Churchill, Birkenhead) and the Baldwinians (Bridgeman, the First Lord, Davidson, the Financial Secretary to the Admiralty, and Amery, Colonial Secretary). In the end Baldwin proffered a compromise and it was accepted. But great damage had been done, not least in dampening down interest in defence research.

'I have always felt', wrote J. C. C. Davidson, 'that Churchill ought to have accepted the collective responsibility of the Cabinet of which he was a member for the deficiencies in defence which the Socialist Government inherited in 1929 and which they did nothing to improve.' For the military deficiencies which so inhibited Baldwin and Britain in the 1930s in their dealings with the dictators, Churchill was much to blame, writes R. A. Butler. Arms and armies are not built in a day, nor in three years, and the dejection Churchill induced in the defence establishments between 1924 and 1929 scarcely worked out of their systems until the mid-1930s.

Baldwin was never a disarmer, as Churchill knew and said in a memo to him on 19 March 1926: 'I know how strong your own views are on the need of a higher concentration of effort in the Fighting Forces.' He saw how faithfully Baldwin chaired the Committee of Imperial Defence after Curzon's death, how determined he was to defend from all encroachment the RAF as a separate service, how he instituted the Joint Planning Committee of the three services to get them to cooperate more closely, how he created the Imperial Defence College.

So why did Baldwin let Churchill do it? Partly because he always gave his Ministers their heads, but more particularly because Churchill's inroads into the Services' money and morale took place in the sunshine flooding over Europe from the balmy Swiss spa of Locarno, where in October 1925 Britain signed a treaty with France, Belgium, Germany and Italy. The King expressed the palmy days mood exactly the morning after Locarno was signed: 'I pray this may mean peace for many years. Why not for ever?' Ironically the ingenious compact at Locarno committed Britain and Italy to declare war without further parley on Germany if Germany attacked France, and to declare war on France if France attacked Germany. The German–Belgian and the German–French frontiers, as fixed at Versailles, were guaranteed inviolable by the five signatories. Austen Chamberlain got most of the lavish praise handed out; Baldwin bulldozed it through the Cabinet, a number of whose members thought the commitment to fight rather than first to consult went far too far, and that Britain would have too little control over consequent events; some of them also disliked tying Britain's fortunes to France's, and wanted Britain to retain her freedom of decision. The Locarno treaty did not mention Germany's frontiers on the east. Worse still, it said nothing about how the guaranteeing, that is the war-making, was to be done. The British Chiefs of Staff received no instructions to plan to implement Locarno. Canada and South Africa were against the treaty, observing that Britain had asserted her national interest against the interest of the Empire.

Few people noticed the discrepancy between Locarno with its explicit military undertakings and the disarmament then being plugged at the League of Nations. Baldwin somehow imagined that Locarno added teeth to one corner of the League of Nation's jaw. Publicly he approved of the League, and even attached a Minister, Lord Robert Cecil, permanently to it in Geneva. Privately neither Baldwin nor his Foreign Secretary Austen Chamberlain thought of it as replacing the old diplomacy. Not without subtlety and certainly with irony, he conveyed his doubts to a meeting in 1928 of the League of Nations Union, that extraordinary amalgam of do-gooders, left-wingers and trendy parsons.

Men were still men, he told them, and as such descended both from the ape and the tiger. To sign a covenant was not enough; hatred must be renounced and he asked that none of his audience should ever 'add one drop to the foetid stream of insinuation and suspicion and the attribution of low motives'. If they truly sought peace, they should start at home: 'Unless a country is at peace with itself, the weight of that country's voice and influence are diminished in the councils of the world.' He emphasized that to be effective the League must be all-embracing – which, without America, it never was.

Baldwin's early doubt of the efficacy of the League had increased since the Corfu affair. In his heart of hearts he feared that there was truth in the views of his close political friend Bridgeman, who in his private diaries during December 1928 noted: 'The only threat to universal peace amongst the great nations seems to me to be the pressures of the League of Nations where international cranks attempt to tie free people by fetters too rigid to be borne.' Among the cranks was Baldwin's own irritable and rash Minister, Cecil, of whom Austen Chamberlain observed that 'being more of a pacifist than I am, he is naturally more prone to forcible methods'. In the end Cecil resigned, leaving the public with the impression that he could not work with the war-mongering Baldwin Government.

As the sun set over Locarno, a red glare rose over the coalfields. In 1925 Baldwin bought off – his own words – a miners' strike by giving a last-minute short-term subsidy. During March and April 1926, he twice brought owners and miners together to seek conciliation, but in vain. A Royal Commission reported; neither side accepted its findings. The miners had a good cause and much public sympathy; for coal face-workers the job was hard, dirty and dangerous. Their wages had risen in 1924 when the Ruhr miners ceased production during the French occupation and British coal was in great demand. But as Baldwin had foreseen, when the Ruhr started work again the demand fell steeply; so did profits, from £59m. in 1923–4 to minus £2.1m. in the first half of 1925. The owners knew only one answer: to cut wages and increase the hours of work. The miners replied: 'Not a penny off pay, not an hour on the day.' Baldwin refused to nationalize, believing that 'the businessman takes risks: the official dare not . . . Business could never therefore show the margin of profit that it shows under private enterprise.' Nor would he for practical reasons coerce the industry, as he had done with the electricity producers, into rationalization, even though he knew that coal was at once the most basic and the most inefficient industry.

The coal subsidy ran out on 30 April and the day after, 1 May, the owners declared a lock-out. The TUC General Council were now handling negotiations for the miners; Baldwin, with Birkenhead and Steel-Maitland, Minister of Labour, were in almost continuous session with them until shortly after midnight on 2–3 May. It was then learned that the TUC had given the go-ahead for a General Strike from the following Sunday and that in fact the printers of the *Daily Mail* had actually started a strike that evening by refusing to print an editorial. Baldwin, worn out by the hours of talk, went to bed; despite half-hearted attempts by the TUC to continue negotiations – at 1.30 am – the strike was on.

Baldwin when he got up on the morning of 4 May was quite clear in mind and decisive in action. The General Strike, he told the Commons that afternoon, was an attempt to take over the function of Government by a body that had not been elected. If they were successful it would be the end of Parliamentary democracy. There could, therefore, be no negotiations. The TUC must surrender. The miners' strike was a separate issue, a trade dispute in the coal industry over which the Government would take the greatest pains in reaching a settlement. Baldwin then activated the Emergency Committee on Supply and Transport, based on the Emergency Powers Act of 1920, and so carefully nurtured by Davidson and John Anderson, Permanent Under-Secretary at the Home Office. Telegrams with the code word 'Action' were dispatched to the Civil Commissioners in the eleven areas into which the country had been divided. Each Commissioner had a staff for finance, food, coal, transport, postal work and shipping, with a police officer and a military liaison officer. In case of violence each Civil Commissioner was to exercise all the powers of Government. The stocks of food and fuel, quietly hoarded long before, were convoyed to their destinations, and water supply, sanitation and gas were ensured. The troops were moved about in full marching order to show the flag. Volunteers belonging to the 'Organization for the Maintenance of Supplies' flocked in to drive lorries, trams, tubes and buses; to act as special constables; and to unload ships at the docks.

If Baldwin had gambled on how the public would react, the

gamble visibly paid off. 'Now', writes the historian of the General Strike, Julian Symons, 'tens of thousands of British citizens . . . found the strike the most enjoyable time of their lives.' Excitement was in the air, comradeship too; the stiff upper lip relaxed and the bowlers and the cloth caps worked side by side. Some 3,350 undergraduates from Cambridge alone were working on buses and in the docks from Hull to Dover and the Superintendent of the Royal Albert Dock said they did the work in sixty per cent of the time the professional dockers would have taken. Some of the amateurs were clumsy and managed to drive trams off their rails, but many were so successful in the jobs for which they had no experience as to destroy the idea that the skilled man is indispensable. Some volunteers from the ranks of the unemployed found the good wages an unmixed blessing. Although there were glimpses of that 'headstrong, moody, murmurous race' that in the past the British had often been, picketing was only sporadic, stone-throwing and baton charges occurred here and there, but there was no real disorder.

Baldwin, contrary to some accounts, was not idle during the strike. Negotiations were out until the TUC withdrew the strike notices but Baldwin made two effective broadcasts, the first on 6 May, appealing to 'all good citizens whose livelihood and labour have thus been put in peril to bear with fortitude and patience the hardships with which they have been so suddenly confronted', and the second two nights later, when he said: 'I am a man of peace. I am longing and working and praying for peace, but I will not surrender the safety and security of the British Constitution. You placed me in power eighteen months ago by the largest majority accorded to my party for many, many years. Have I done anything to forfeit your confidence? Cannot you trust me to ensure a square deal to secure even justice between man and man?'

He himself drafted and redrafted a notice 'To workers in all trades', which finally read: 'When the present General Strike is ended, H.M. Government will take effectual measures to prevent the victimization by trade unions of any man who remains at work or who may return to work; and no settlement will be agreed to by H.M. Government which does not provide for this for a lasting period and for its enforcement, if necessary, by penalties. No man who does his duty loyally to the country in the present crisis will be left unprotected by the State from subsequent reprisals.' There were one or two in his Cabinet who advocated more dramatic methods than merely to wait for the strike to wear itself out. One of them was Churchill, the Chancellor of the Exchequer, whom Baldwin skilfully side-tracked into editing the *British Gazette*, the official Government paper, although he there behaved as though 'he thought he was Napoleon'. 'Curiously enough,' wrote Davidson, 'the men who have been printing all their life in the various processes happen to know more about their jobs than he does.' Julian Symons adds his tribute: 'Baldwin's management of the conflicting forces inside the Cabinet was masterly ... wonderfully light and dexterous and to him, more than to any other individual, must go credit for the pacific conduct of the strike.'

Baldwin had his fears. He suspected that MacDonald, the leader of the Labour Party, 'was a Kerenski and the Kerenskis have lost control', and that Ernest Bevin, of the Transport and General Workers, might 'picture himself as the Napoleon of the trade union movement'. Such fears proved groundless, yet in the context they were not unjustified. Even before the Zinoviev letter, Baldwin had been aware of Communist penetration in the guise of the Minority Movement into the trade unions; he remembered the General Secretary of the Communist-sponsored International Labour Union in August 1925, at Derby, explaining exactly how civil upheaval was to be provoked, and he had read of a Communist veteran, Tom Mann, encouraging 'unremitting and relentless war on the British Empire for its downfall'. He knew that as soon as the strike began the Russians offered the TUC a gift of 2m. roubles which, however, the TUC politely turned down.

This undercurrent of subversion was weak and ineffective, though Baldwin could not have known that at the time. The General Strike was never whole-heartedly supported by most leaders of the Labour Party and the trade unions. It languished and was officially called off on 12 May. The TUC made its peace with the Government and left the miners to fend for themselves. So much for fraternal solidarity. On the evening of the 12th Baldwin again broadcast, emphasizing that 'our business is not to triumph over those who have failed in a mistaken attempt', and promising negotiations without delay to 'adjust differences between owner and miner'. Baldwin received much praise for 'cooling' the strike, and the Cabinet placed on record their

appreciation of the part his reputation had played in the uncon-
ditional withdrawal of the strike notices.

But what happened to his aim of bringing together all classes
of people, which he had declared to be 'the main end and object
of my life in politics'? He confessed to the Commons: 'I know I
shall be told: this is the end of all your dreamy visionary speeches
about peace and all that kind of thing. Let me say this: I have
worked for two years to the utmost of my ability in one direction.
I have failed so far. That does not take away from me either my
faith or my courage ... Before long the angel of peace, with
healing in his wings, will be among us again ... I shall start again
... I know that the seed that I have tried to plant in men's hearts
these two years is germinating.'

His faith and his courage were indisputable: the General Strike,
as he had handled it, cleared the air of whatever revolutionary
current it had contained. It was the first and last general strike in
Britain. For long the unions were in no position to support strikes
since their membership fell by half a million and their funds from
£12½m. to £8½m. a year. Everyday life returned to normal with
remarkable ease.

What was in doubt was Baldwin's physical and mental strength
once the crisis was over. He tried through endless talks with the
miners and the owners to bring about a compromise settlement,
but he had lost his touch. He let die the one idea which, while
avoiding the pitfalls of nationalization, would have enabled the
coal industry to be organized on a national basis: this was to form
a national holding company with a group of coalowners. It is true
that both miners and owners were unfortunate in their representatives. A. J. Cook was a ranting Marxist; while, as Birkenhead
remarked, he had thought the miners' leaders the most stupid men
he had ever met, until he met the owners. Even so, there were
opportunities Baldwin could have seized had he not fallen into a
sort of nerveless apathy.

He did not make sure, as he had promised, that there would be
no victimization of those who had continued to work during the
strike. He acquiesced too easily in the demand in the Cabinet
and from many of the public for tighter controls to be imposed on
the unions by means of a Trade Disputes and Trade Union Act
which was brought in during 1927. This declared a general strike
illegal and enforced 'contracting in' for the unions' political levy,

the very thing he had vetoed so firmly in the MacQuisten bill. Baldwin now defended this as stemming from the unions' actions of the previous year and, he pointed out, the Government had not been the first to fire a shot. The Trade Disputes Bill caused uproar in the House and Snowden asked how the Government would propose to imprison five million men. It was forced through by the huge Conservative majority and it undoubtedly damaged Baldwin's reputation as a moderate man. One Labour member described him as 'the greatest enemy of the working class in the present generation'. Another member, promptly suspended, called him a murderer.

Throughout this post-strike period Baldwin often seemed *distrait*; he was, Tom Jones noted, 'utterly without resource . . . very tired and has rather lost interest in politics'. He became forgetful. He had agreed when Neville Chamberlain wished to include a constructive clause in the Trade Disputes Act which would provide for a sixty-day cooling-off period in any industrial dispute, and compulsory arbitration. A few days later he had forgotten all about it and, Chamberlain told his sister while they were talking over the matter, 'I saw he'd gone out of gear. He started sniffing blotting-paper. He had a way of sniffing blotting-paper when he wasn't paying attention.'

Baldwin's judgement, thought Jones, was warped, and he became irritable, particularly as he was also suffering from lumbago. He would not take a holiday until Jones and Mrs Baldwin plotted together to get a doctor to order him to do so. (Incidentally the only doctor they could find, it being Sunday, was a gynaecologist, who played his part well.) Again a few months later Baldwin was suddenly taken ill when leaving a dinner at the Royal College of Surgeons. He was helped home and put to bed. The doctors reported that there was nothing organically wrong but they insisted that he should go to Chequers and rest in bed. 'I have never been laid up in this way before and I hope I shan't again,' he plaintively wrote to the King's Secretary. It was during this period that he referred to premiership as being 'the loneliest job in the world . . . He must possess his soul in patience and must harden himself to be indifferent to daily criticism.'

He was soon back in Downing Street but was bored by interminable talk in the Cabinet about a reform of the House of Lords by which part of the Lords were to be nominated by the Government of the day and part elected by the peers with power to force an appeal to the country in all cases of difference with the Commons. He once walked out of a Cabinet meeting when the subject was being discussed and offered only a languid defence of the reform when it came up in the House of Commons. The proposal passed into oblivion. He did, however, raise sufficient energy to stamp out yet another attempt to distribute RAF units among the other two services, and thus finally established the independence of the RAF under its own Service ministry.

Baldwin was wearying of his colleagues and of his party generally. He once exclaimed in exasperation: 'My party. What is my party? Diamond Jubilee diehards and Tory democrats pulling me both ways at once.' He was relieved to get away in August for a nineteen-day tour of Canada, then celebrating the 60th anniversary of her Dominion status. On part of his Canadian tour he was accompanied by the Prince of Wales; Baldwin later told the King that the Prince 'was at his best and it was a real pleasure as well as honour to be with him'. The Prince was not so enchanted with his travelling companion, at least not when he – and his 'ghosts' – came to write *A King's Story*, nearly thirty years later. While he approved of Baldwin's conversational gifts on such subjects as 'the apple husbandry of Worcestershire, cricket and the revision of the Prayer Book', he thought that the further they penetrated Canada the more he detected in Baldwin 'traces of the arrogance that some Englishmen display when travelling abroad . . . he became the embodiment of old John Bull himself'. But by the time he wrote that he had abdicated the throne, with Baldwin as master of ceremonies. The tour itself was no holiday; Baldwin made twenty-two speeches in a fortnight, confining himself largely to non-controversial subjects. He was, however, lyrical about the country itself: 'One who visits Canada and sees her in the radiance and glory of her morning, learns a new security,' he said later.

The arrogance the Prince claimed to have discovered in Baldwin went unnoticed by others. Robert Vansittart who, as his principal Private Secretary for two years, daily saw him close-up said memorably that Baldwin 'gave himself nothing, not even airs'. To the public he presented himself 'as a countryman, plain and sensible almost to imbecility'; this, Tom Jones thought, began in contrast to the swaggering, brilliant personae projected by Lloyd George, Birkenhead and Churchill. Jones judged that after the bravado of the Coalitionists, the ordinary man wanted a return to a quieter, more comfortable and secure way of life, and Baldwin symbolized it. Nor was it a conscious pose: at times he was all he looked. Of course, H. J. Laski, Chairman of the Labour Party, was right in saying that 'a simple man has never been Prime Minister of England', but wrong to add that 'his pigs and his pipe are simply the technique of propaganda. Like the orchid of Mr Chamberlain or the ringlets of Disraeli, they create an image which the multitude can remember.' So they did, but it was no deliberate technique such as was employed by a later Prime Minister who puffed a pipe in public and smoked cigars in private.

It was facile to swing the other way and regard Baldwin as 'disguised as an open book' and to claim that he was really the 'subtlest Celt who ever played the complete Englishman', in Vansittart's words. Close colleagues of the time did not think Baldwin subtle, at least not in the derogatory sense applied to the princes of the Renaissance courts. To such a colleague as Amery, he appeared to have a 'slow-moving, hesitant and suspicious mind', yet to hold the 'genuine personal affection of colleagues and followers, often baffled and perplexed by his vagaries in action – or, more often, inaction'.

Baldwin's character had many dimensions. Some friends considered him to be more a sensitive artist than either subtle politician or simple countryman. His ear for words written or spoken was acute. He distrusted jargon, asking his left-wing opponents in the Commons to be kind enough to put into literal English their favourite phrases such as 'the democratic control of the means of production', or 'self-determination', or 'making the world safe for democracy'. No reply. He was at ease with scholars and poets; in music he found solace, and such performers as Myra Hess, the pianist, were frequent guests at Chequers. From his uncles he had learned to appreciate pictures. Once, addressing a group of artists, he drew an amusing analogy between their job and his. 'Your instruments are dumb – pencils and paints. Ours are neither dumb nor inert. I often think that we rather resemble Alice in Wonderland, who tried to play croquet with a flamingo instead of a mallet.' Contemporary art did not entrance him. When he unveiled Epstein's *Rima*, the Hyde Park memorial to W. H. Hudson, he was observed to recoil slightly and forget the customary bow to the sculptor. He did not recoil alone.

There was a tinge of levity in him – or at any rate light-heartedness. In one of his daily Prime Ministerial letters to the King, he wrote of members at a late-night sitting 'lying about the benches in recumbent positions, some being overcome with sleep oblivious of their surroundings', and noted resemblances to St James's Park at midday. The King's Private Secretary, Lord Stamfordham, primly wrote back that the King found the situation 'hardly decorous', particularly as there were lady members.

These reports by Baldwin 'with his humble duty to Your Majesty' are consistently delightful, even impish. On 18 April 1928 there was a discussion in the House on cowardice. Labour, Baldwin reported, 'felt that if it is possible to go to such lengths of definition to state that a horse includes a mule, it should not overtax the ingenuity of the Army Council to define cowardice. In point of fact it is, of course, impossible'. And again, on the siting of petrol pumps: 'The whole House felt that in order to proceed at a fast pace it was not necessary to gaze upon multi-coloured petrol pumps at short intervals. All of which is submitted by Your Majesty's humble, obedient servant.'

Baldwin could be good fun. Once handed a note of a by-election victory at Rotherham, he recalled 'being in the gents on the platform at Rotherham station. The closet seat was square. On the wall were inscribed the words'

> Square seats don't seem to bother 'em,
> They've got some rum bums in Rotherham.

The years 1924 to 1937 have been described as the Baldwin age but, except that Baldwin was for thirteen years its modestly prominent political leader, the age was not his nor he its. He was a mid-Victorian whose first thirty-four years had passed in the time of the old Queen: what had the novelties of the 1920s and 1930s – the speculations of Bertrand Russell and Professor Eddington, the 'Black Bottom' and the '43', the Bauhaus and art déco, the music of Walton and Duke Ellington, the galloping growth of hire purchase and dirt-track racing, to do with him or he with them? Women bobbed their hair and then Eton-cropped it and their hats became toques or bandeaux; but not Mrs Baldwin, whose hats were more surrealist than Hans Arp's paintings. Some men affected Oxford bags and Fair Isle sweaters and two-tone shoes but Mr Baldwin wore baggy suits and old-fashioned wing-collars. Modernities Baldwin scarcely noticed, like the Babies' Ball, Aimée Semple Macpherson, *The Well of Loneliness*, and the new electric cookers, which were to him a dream sequence unrolling on a dim screen at which he seldom glanced. But the debunking young often glanced at him; he was a national anachronism, and the progressives (including his own son, Oliver) needed to show just how advanced they were in contrast to the home-loving, pipe-smoking, sober fuddy-duddy King's First Minister.

Cars now thronged the roads like tinny beetles; Baldwin seldom entered one without a *crise de nerfs*. He saw the skies filling with airliners of Imperial Airways but he never ventured aboard, amazed at the courage of the young Amy Johnson flying alone to Australia. 'Speed', Baldwin once observed, 'has become the God of our civilization, but don't think it is synonymous with civilization.' Speed, he told the Federation of British Industry, was also responsible for the 'nervous breakdown', an ailment unheard of fifty years before, but now common 'from the chairman of the greatest company in the kingdom down to the workman of the lowest grade.'

That newish miracle, wireless, Baldwin studied as a speaker, once asking its director, John Reith, whether working men listened at home or in pubs; there is no evidence that he ever 'listened in' to the late-night dance music transmitted by the Savoy Orpheans or by Henry Hall from Gleneagles Hotel, or to Capt. H. B. T. Wakelam's commentaries on Rugby football matches, or to Flotsam and Jetsam or to such 'shocking' plays as Reginald Berkeley's *The White Chateau*. He visited the theatre, generally to see musical comedies rather than the 'trendy' plays of Noel Coward or of Shaw. He thought there ought to be more British films shown though he seldom went to the cinema: there had been no commercial cinema until he was nearly forty. He liked watching cricket and the Cambridge crew practising for the boat race ('not one of them wants even an O.B.E.'); he played a little tennis but he neither hunted, shot or fished, thus lessening his value as an Aunt Sally. His passion was still for reading, voraciously and haphazardly, taking in, of his own time, Hardy, his cousin Kipling, Conrad, probably Bennett and Wells, certainly the poetry of T. S. Eliot and the thrillers of Edgar Wallace and such highly personal choices as Mary Webb and Helen Waddell, but probably not Virginia Woolf or Waugh. In a sense, statistically, it *was* the literary age of Baldwin: there were more readers who read the sort of thing he did than read James Joyce or the Sitwells, or, at first, D. H. Lawrence.

Church and chapel attendance was falling steeply, so Baldwin was not typical of his age, for he was a regular churchgoer. To him, however, religion did not depend on outward form: prayer and contemplation were in his heart, rather than in his pew. He showed little interest in establishment Anglicanism or the revision of the Prayer Book which caused such a fuss in 1928. He was never 'churchy'. Baldwin's was a great age of science, in which, unlike his predecessors Balfour and the great Lord Salisbury, he had small apparent interest; yet he knew something of what was going on in 1932, which C. P. Snow has called 'the most spectacular year in the history of science', when the atom was split, an act that would in due course radically alter war, politics and diplomacy. Baldwin told Tom Jones in 1933 that he had been to Cambridge 'to hear them bombard the electrons'; he even vaguely knew that scientific men could in theory make a bomb about the size of a walnut with devastating power. He had caught a glimpse of the Freudian revolution: 'Nor is conscience dead,' he once told the Congregational Union, 'though modern psychologists call it by another name' (doubtless the 'super-ego'). Certainly he had heard of that other semi-scientific revolution, birth control, led by Dr Marie Stopes, though, unlike certain of his Parliamentary colleagues, he would not comprehend the mechanics of the contraceptive she advocated.

The new age passed Baldwin by and he passed it up, because though, as Guedalla put it, he sat among the red boxes at Westminster and sighed for the English countryside, he was absorbed by politics and what his contemporary F. S. Oliver called the endless adventure of ruling men, and he had time for little else. What impress he had on his period was purely political, with perhaps one exception, and that arose partly from politics. Baldwin's policies had gone far towards creating that familiar stereotype of the period, 'the little man'. He was born out of the fall in the cost of living resulting from the return to the gold standard and from the sense of stability following the quiet demise of the General Strike.

For all but the chronically unemployed, life in the late 1920s improved and was full of hope. The lower and lower middle classes became mildly prosperous and rather 'comfy', a vogue word they used among themselves. They lived in the new little houses, often on one of the estates speculative builders were erecting outside the towns, resulting in that disfigurement known as 'ribbon development'. They were snug, they kept themselves to themselves and their paterfamilias was the cartoonist Strube's little man, bewildered by politics but content to smoke his pipe and, after work, to potter in his tiny garden. In his Sunday tweed jacket he might venture down the leafy street for half a pint before the roast beef and Yorkshire pudding.

Money was still short but now there was enough, prudently laid out, to provide a regular life with adequate heating, lighting, bathing and food and enough over for modest replenishments of wardrobes and two weeks by the sea in August. The little man's children, if they were bright, went to one of the excellent grammar schools or to the scarcely less excellent secondary schools. Sometimes the family trotted off to the cinema, sometimes father and sons visited a soccer match, but regular entertainment came via the wireless with its apparently immemorial nine o'clock news, its dance music, its vaudeville and its plays. What reason to go out with such entertainment at home? The lives of the little men of suburbia sounded dull and in-growing to the well-to-do or the intellectuals, but to those newly emancipated from hand-to-mouth existence it was a bliss they would never regard as stuffy, and would not willingly forego.

The little man owed something to Baldwin, and in however diminished a form, to the public image of Baldwin's way of life. The real Baldwin he scarcely at all resembled.

5
MACDONALD'S HEAD MAN
1929–1935

THE BALDWIN GOVERNMENT'S glad, confident morning was fading into dreary night by the beginning of 1928. The Prime Minister was to be seen limping through the lobbies with the aid of a stick – he had had a bad fall at Chequers over Christmas 1927 – and his Government seemed to limp with him. He was testy with Conservative back-benchers whose attendance was slack and with his colleagues. 'Every morning,' he said, 'I am full of hope, faith and cheer. By lunchtime, I've lost a great deal of it and by evening I've given up all hope of this world and the next.'

What frustrated Baldwin most was that his Government's ameliorative policies were not working fast enough, so that in July 1928 the unemployed had risen by 278,000 to 1,305,000. The workless were mainly in cotton, steel, coal and building. Brusquely Baldwin told these industries to get rid of 'uneconomic elements' and reduce capacity to a competitive level, which meant more unemployment until such time as the new industries of the Midlands and the South got under way, and he saw no means of easing the transition apart from urging Norman at the Bank of England to intervene with loans to industry. Meanwhile, he was saddened by despairing reports from the Industrial Transference Board of the appalling plight of the depressed areas.

Baldwin's tired colleagues ventured their mutually contradictory advice. The Protectionist Dominions Secretary Amery told him: 'You ought to reconstitute the Cabinet (not the whole Ministry) before the election. We may or may not be stale in our job but the public thinks so . . . The essential thing is to move Winston . . . In

84

The Harrow schoolboy – Stanley Baldwin at seventeen.

THIS PAGE
TOP Baldwin's mother, Louisa, whose Celtic ancestry produced, in Baldwin's words, '. . . the erratic creature that is me . . .'. She loved and practised the arts publishing romantic novels, ghost stories, poems and children's tales.
BOTTOM Baldwin's father, Alfred, with the Board of Directors of Baldwins Ltd., from whom **he** inherited his nervousness, but also his self-control, devoutness, strong will and intelligence.

OPPOSITE PAGE
TOP A picture taken in 1917 showing *left to right* Philip Burne-Jones (Baldwin's cousin), Rudyard (Baldwin's cousin) and Carrie Kipling, Baldwin, Margot Baldwin, Diana Baldwin, and Elsie Kipling.
BOTTOM The Baldwins on holiday in Aix-les-Bains with their friends John and Joan (Mimi) Davidson.

Stanley Baldwin   W. Charles Wright   Roger Beck   Samuel Dore

Aubrey Butler

John Roper Wright   Alfred Baldwin   Isaac Butler

First Board of Directors of Baldwins Ltd.
1902

TOP LEFT Watching the cricket at
Chequers during Baldwin's first
term of office.
TOP RIGHT Baldwin with Lord
Curzon on the eve of the Resignation
of the Government in 1924.
BOTTOM LEFT Baldwin with Joseph
Oakes during the ceremony in which
he received the Freedom of Bewdley
in 1925.
BOTTOM RIGHT The Prime
Minister with Tom Jones during
negotiations with miners'
representatives in July, 1925.

THIS PAGE
TOP The Baldwins at Ascot in 1926.
BOTTOM Oliver Baldwin, the Prime Minister's elder son, pictured during the Election in 1929 when he was a successful Labour Candidate.

OPPOSITE PAGE
TOP Baldwin electioneering with Ramsay MacDonald and Sir John Simon in 1931.
BOTTOM The Ottawa Delegates aboard the 'Empress of Britain' in 1932. *Left to right* (seated) J. H. Thomas, Baldwin, Neville Chamberlain, (standing) Sir Philip Cunliffe-Lister, the first Lord Hailsham, Walter Runciman, and Sir John Gilmour.

TOP Baldwin in the kitchen garden of his home, Astley Hall, Worcestershire.
BOTTOM LEFT Edward VIII with the Prime Minister just before the Abdication crisis.
BOTTOM RIGHT The Baldwins in Aix-les-Bains with Anthony Eden and J. P. L. Thomas after Eden's resignation in 1938.

spite of all his brilliancy and verbal originality, he is entirely lacking in constructive thought and imagination in the economic field. A paralysing negative influence.' Rather, Amery suggested, entrust him with the coordinating of the fighting services or the Foreign Office where 'Austen is wearying'. No sooner had Amery ceased than Churchill opened up: 'I am for "the old cause and the new lot". I am sure it would be wise to refresh the team *before* the match and not too long before. Painful, worrying but safer . . . Without a stream of new talent we cannot hold our ascendancy. We don't want to be left alone with Jix and Amery.'

Baldwin was no butcher. The only major changes he made were brought about by death or retirement. Birkenhead left the India Office in 1928, partly for health reasons (he died in 1930), partly to recoup his finances. Baldwin had grown quite to like him because, as Bridgeman noted in his diary, 'his mind in spite of his potations was always clear and he would come to a morning meeting looking perfectly shattered and suddenly produce the most lucid contribution of the day'. The grandee Marquis of Londonderry became Minister of Works and, as Birkenhead put it, began 'catering his way to the Cabinet'.

Baldwin dissolved Parliament in early May 1929. Davidson as Party Chairman fluttered round him like an admiring hen (in the words of Salvidge, the Liverpool party boss) and ran a misguided campaign. He plugged the slogan suggested by an advertising agency, 'Safety First', then being used in a drive against road accidents. Baldwin did not care for it. He was also portrayed on thousands of posters as 'the man you can trust'. Davidson bought cinema vans and, for the first time, sent a campaign guide to candidates; he distributed the ridiculous election song written by Waldron Smithers and based on Al Jolson's 'talkie' song, 'Sonny Boy':

> Whatever they may say, Sir
> You will never stray, Sir,
> For we love you so!
> *Stanley Boy!*

Davidson had plenty of money in the party chest, much of it raised from the City, and he spent £300,000. But he had sacked the Principal Agent, which did not make for Central Office harmony, and given women high posts in the party, which enraged club-land Tories.

Baldwin, campaigning, progressed through the country like royalty. He promised no panaceas. He asked for trust. He offered the mixture as before. But the patient did not want the medicine. Convalescent now, stable, almost buoyant, he wanted change. This the Liberals alone seemed to offer, now that Lloyd George had plastered over their party cracks. They put forward new and cogent ideas for solving unemployment in their manifestos *Britain's Industrial Future* and *We Can Conquer Unemployment*; they were the 'new frontiersmen' of their day. Baldwin tartly observed: 'It is no new thing for the party of performance to be charged with an inadequate programme.'

The election result shocked Baldwin. He had appealed to the people to trust him and they had refused! The Conservative vote was over 8½ m., giving 260 seats, but Labour with under 8½m. votes got 288 seats, while the Liberal Party with more than 5½m. votes had only 59 seats. The situation was 1923 all over again except that for the first time Labour was the largest single party. What would Baldwin do? 'I found him', wrote Jones, 'in a state of great nervous tension, the L.G. obsession weighing heavily on his mind.' He could remain in office with Liberal support but his detestation of Lloyd George stopped that. Lloyd George, he foresaw, would sport with him, keep him in office for a week or a month 'and humiliate him and his party in every conceivable way'.

Four days after defeat Baldwin went to Windsor and resigned. Immediately his spirits rose, 'his nervousness gone because his mind was made up'. Two days later Baldwin and his wife set off house-hunting. Without his Prime Ministerial salary and no dividends from Baldwins Ltd., he took a small house in Upper Brook Street through the Duke of Westminster's agent. Even Astley might have to be let or sold. 'The financial cloud depresses me beyond words,' wrote Mrs Baldwin in her diary. One consolation was that the alienated Oliver, Baldwin's elder son, now a Labour MP, wrote to him, in a warm and compassionate way. 'More like his old self, thank God,' wrote his mother in her diary.

Defeat was succeeded by inquests. The 'flapper' vote – flapper was the vogue term for young single women – was not thought to be a factor, though the Conservatives got no credit for their Equal Franchise Act, which for the first time gave the vote to women of twenty-one, against the strong protestations of backwoods Conservatives. The fairest assessment was made by Bridgeman in his diary:

The election was lost, not, I think, from any wave of resentment against the Government and certainly not against Baldwin, nor on any one particular piece of policy or legislation. Of the items which together produced our defeat, I put the love of change common to all democracies ... as the first after that, the coincidence of reassessment with the De-rating Bill which greatly prejudiced the latter, the cry of 'Safety First', the rather lukewarm action of past years in Safeguarding, the failure of most candidates to explain the Derating Bill and failure of most candidates to put it forward, as it ought to have been, as a winning card, and the wild promises of Liberals and Labour ... widows' pensions did us little good, as there is no gratitude in political contests.

The Tory party was not going to take defeat lying down, so, and as is their custom, they turned to rend their leader. Baldwin expected the backlash. He had after all lost his power of patronage and some of his followers had lost their seats. All his Ministers had lost office and some concerned themselves with little else than inching into good positions for the next period in power which, as during the first Labour Government, seemed unlikely to be long delayed. Labour, unprepared for office, staggered from compromise to compromise in what Baldwin called their 'Socialist palace of promises', and unemployment rose in a steady curve. All over the world trade slumped, prices of primary products fell, huge tariff walls were built with the urgency of besieged armies digging in.

Beaverbrook thought he knew the answer – Empire Free Trade, which was part of his old dream of an Empire closing its ranks against the rest of the world, and he dearly wanted to get Baldwin on his side. Baldwin was not unsympathetic but saw too many drawbacks: food taxes, those the public would never stand for, and, what killed the policy stone dead, the Dominion Governments unanimously declared against Empire Free Trade. They had chosen to become industrial bastions behind their own tariff walls and Britain could not reverse their decision. Undaunted, Beaverbrook, aided some of the time by the other Press Lord, Rothermere, went ahead without Baldwin, formed a United Empire party, put up candidates who won some by-elections, and drew much support from all ranks of the Conservative party, particularly the younger members, to whom his newspapers and those of Rothermere ceaselessly poured out their propaganda.

Here, then, was a serious threat to Baldwin's leadership. He moved swiftly by calling a party meeting of MPs and candidates, and there, on 24 June 1930, he cut the Beaverbrook-Rothermere faction to pieces and sternly exhorted his audience: 'We are told that there is a crisis in the party . . . there will be a crisis if you cannot make up your minds. I have made up my mind but you have got to make up yours. You have been told that we have no policy. We have a policy that I have been explaining up and down the country.' Then he turned to the Press Lords and here, as he afterwards confessed, the Lord had been kind to him. Beaverbrook and Rothermere sought, he said, to dictate policy to a big party, as had the TUC in 1926, to choose a leader, to impose Ministers on the Crown. He read out a letter from Rothermere saying he would not support Baldwin 'unless I have complete guarantees that such a policy [i.e. Empire Free Trade] will be carried out if his party achieves office and unless I am acquainted beforehand with the names of at least eight or ten prominent colleagues in the next Ministry'. Baldwin paused to let the words sink in. Then: 'Those are the terms that your leader would have to accept and when sent for by the King, would have to say, "Sire, these names are not necessarily my choice, but they have the support of Lord Rothermere." A more preposterous and insolent demand was never made on the leader of any political party. I repudiate it with contempt and I will fight that attempt at domination to the end.'

Baldwin walked into the Chamber that afternoon to an immense ovation, even more prolonged from the Labour benches than his own. His old Socialist admirer, Laski, wrote to him that many Socialists, recognizing his 'human directness' and his contribution to the 'peaceful evolution of English politics', resented the effort to usurp his distinguished and honoured leadership. But once more, in October 1930, Baldwin had to address a party meeting. 'Photograph me now, gentlemen,' he said to press photographers at the entrance to Carlton Hall, 'it may be the last time you will see me.' On the contrary, the meeting passed a vote of confidence in him, 462 to 116.

Surprisingly, it was India, wrote the back-bench Conservative Winterton, that 'nearly blew that tough old oak [Baldwin] out of the leadership'. Baldwin had long believed that India must be guided into self-government and towards eventual Dominion status, and to the ideas of 'majorities and minorities, of checks and balances, of local freedom and federal union'. To him this would be the final achievement of English Imperial justice. This was why he had sent out Irwin (formerly Wood, later Halifax) as Viceroy, because his 'ideals and views in political life approximate most closely to my own'. Now, in December 1930, after years of bombs and riots, Irwin's conciliatory policy seemed to be working: the Indian princes declared themselves ready to join in an all-India federal scheme. This strengthened faith in Indian political maturity, and responsible self-government seemed to be around the next but one corner. Baldwin was delighted, so was the Labour Government. Many, perhaps most, Conservatives were not, among them Churchill. He raged through the country talking of Britain's 'hideous act of self-mutilation . . . casting away that most truly bright and precious jewel in the crown of the King', and demanding that Gandhi's evil philosophy be crushed – 'it is no use trying to satisfy a tiger by feeding it on cat's meat'. On 26 January 1931, Churchill left the Conservative Shadow Cabinet.

Baldwin's dreamy idealism over India – just as unrealistic as Churchill's dogma – split his party and once more his leadership was at risk. Mutterings, buzzings were heard; backstairs meetings took place. Baldwin asked Derby: 'Tell me as an old friend, do you think I ought to resign?' Derby replied: 'Well, old man, I hate to say it but I think you ought.' Neville Chamberlain, who had succeeded Davidson as Chairman of the Party, doubted whether Baldwin could remain, but could not tell him so because he was the heir-apparent. But there were roundabout ways of doing so and one now came to hand. This was a memorandum to Chamberlain from the Principal Agent Sir Robert Topping, who reported that Central Office colleagues and party officials in the country feared that Baldwin could not win another election; he 'should reconsider his position'. It is clear now that Topping had deliberately exaggerated the discontent, had consulted mainly the activists and discounted resolutions in support of Baldwin which were arriving daily from the constituencies.

Chamberlain, however, seized upon the memorandum and sent it round to Baldwin at Upper Brook Street on Sunday morning, 1 March. Hot foot after lunch Chamberlain himself arrived, agog. With many expressions of regret he told Baldwin that he and a number of his colleagues thought he should resign. Chamberlain expected Baldwin to delay. He was therefore astonished when Baldwin coolly said: 'Very well, the sooner the better. Let's have a meeting of my colleagues tomorrow morning when I can say "goodbye".' Chamberlain sped away to Central Office; shortly afterwards *The Times* had an article set up in type and headed 'Mr Baldwin withdraws'. Meanwhile Baldwin asked Davidson and Bridgeman to come and see him. They arrived after dinner, Bridgeman blowing in like an admiral in a gale. They found the Baldwins 'quite convinced that they were about to retire from politics altogether and retreat to their home in Worcestershire where they looked forward to a period of complete leisure'. So, said Mrs Baldwin, 'we four were together at the beginning of Stanley's leadership and now we're together for the farewell'.

'Farewell be damned,' said Bridgeman. Stand and fight, he advised, and why not do it on a challenge to the 'right of the press millionaires to dictate procedure to the party'? Opportunity offered at a by-election pending in St George's, Westminster. Beaverbrook was putting up a candidate and, humiliatingly, Moore-Brabazon, the Conservative, had withdrawn rather than defend Baldwin. Why should not Baldwin seek the Chiltern Hundreds and put himself up for St George's? Baldwin liked the idea, startling as it was; if he won handsomely it would be one in the eye for the Press Lords; if he lost he could retire with honour, championing the right cause. Yes, said Mrs Baldwin enthusiastically, muttering 'Tiger Baldwin', and yes, said Baldwin, hastily despatching a note summoning Chamberlain for the morrow.

When Chamberlain arrived next day, Baldwin was steely, for he had heard rumours of Chamberlain's plottings. 'I have decided to go down fighting and I propose to be adopted as the official candidate for St George's.' 'S.B., you can't do that,' said Chamberlain, with a look of surprise. 'Why not?' 'Think of the effect on your successor.' 'I don't give a damn about my successor.' Well might *The Times* write that Baldwin's 'spiritual home is always the last ditch'. He was, for once, angry. He doubted whether Chamberlain as Party Chairman had been very vigorous in his cause. He doubted still more when Davidson told him that Topping was motivated by his 'own personal hostility to me – a pretty state of affairs' and that he was reflecting the aims of his chairman, Chamberlain.

Coolly as he dealt with Chamberlain, Baldwin was excited. 'I love a crisis,' he once said. Narrating the sequence of events to Jones ten days later, Jones wrote in his diary: 'I could see he was excited from the frequent twitching of his facial muscles and from his voluble talk . . . Frequently he got up and paced the room, tapping the floor with his feet excitedly . . . ' Could he, the Prime Minister, give up his own constituency, and fight a by-election elsewhere? In the end, he did not have to do so. A champion armed cap-à-pie charged forward in the very personable person of Alfred Duff Cooper, aged fifty, a Conservative who had been nursing the safe seat of Winchester. He offered himself as the pro-Baldwin candidate at St George's and was accepted. The game was not yet won. Only reluctantly did Neville Chamberlain put the Central Office behind Duff Cooper. Even the usually optimistic Mrs Baldwin wrote in her diary: 'Things are getting difficult. I wonder how much more we can bear.'

Fortunately, at this point, 12 March, Baldwin was required to speak in the Commons during the India debate, and had a great success. He withdrew none of his views on India's future but he explained his attitude in glowing, challenging words. 'If there are those in our party who approach this subject in a niggling, grudging spirit, who would have to have forced out of their reluctant hands one concession after another, if they be a majority, in God's name let them choose a man to lead them. If they are in a minority, then let them at least refrain from throwing difficulties in the way of those who have undertaken an almost superhuman task, on the successful fulfillment of which depends the well-being, the prosperity and the duration of the whole British Empire.' He was cheered to the echo. A week later he chalked up another success in words that have never been forgotten. The *Daily Mail*, supporting the Empire Crusade candidate at the St George's by-election, attacked Baldwin personally. He was accused of having dissipated the immense fortune left him by his father and was asked how it could be that the leader of a party who had 'lost his own fortune can hope to restore that of anyone else, or of his own country'.

To this Baldwin replied in a speech supporting Duff Cooper at the by-election. He damned the Beaverbrook–Rothermere papers as 'engines of propaganda' and then turned to the personal passage in the *Mail*: 'The paragraph', he said, 'could only have been written by a cad,' and since it was untrue, he had been told that an action for libel would lie. 'Take it!' shouted a voice from the hall. No, said Baldwin, 'I shall not move in the matter and for this reason – I should get an apology and heavy damages. The first is of no value, and the second I would not touch with a barge pole. What the proprietorship of these papers is aiming at is power and power without responsibility – the prerogative of the harlot throughout the ages.' The reporters, Lady Diana Duff Cooper wrote, jumped out of their skins at the harsh phrase (which Kipling had suggested to his cousin).

This speech, followed by Duff Cooper's 5,000 majority, made Baldwin the impregnable leader of the party and marked the end of Empire Free Trade as an effective political force. Beaverbrook said: 'He always beats me – the toughest and most unscrupulous politician you could find – cold, merciless in his dislikes.' One or two things remained for Baldwin to tidy up. Neville Chamberlain had resigned the party chairmanship but now they shook hands 'with the clouds removed'. Austen Chamberlain still niggled away about Baldwin's 'apparent inertia and lack of incisiveness', but this simply made people laugh in a month that had seen Baldwin scatter his enemies and impose on his party a policy over India that many of them heartily disliked. In later years Baldwin used to speak with a shy little smile of 1931 as 'the year my party tried to get rid of me'. How had he won? Because, Churchill wrote a few years later, he had the 'phlegmatic capacity of putting up with a score of unpleasant and even humbling situations in order to be master of something very big at the end of a blue moon'. It is as good an explanation as any other.

By the early summer of 1931 the MacDonald Government were in such trouble, and the country with them, that they began to panic. J. H. Thomas, the Minister charged with solving the unemployment problem, symbolized their posture; he was seen after a vinous Mansion House luncheon slumped over the table 'hysterical in his outbursts of self-pity', and, according to his colleague Arthur Henderson, the Foreign Secretary, 'bordering on lunacy'. At the time the insured unemployed had risen to a dizzy 2.6 million and the total figure of workless was near 3.3 million. As a result the Unemployment Insurance Fund was in debt and survived only by State borrowing.

This was only part of the grim tale. British exports halved between 1929 and 1931, mainly as a distant consequence of the crash of the United States stock market and the resulting scramble for liquidity, which caused the withdrawal of deposits from London and elsewhere. The British balance of payments deteriorated and was not 'corrected' as usually in the past by the 'invisible' items such as banking, shipping and interest on foreign investments, for these were the hardest hit by the world depression. City bankers had borrowed from French depositors to help Germany; now, because of tension between France and Germany, the French withdrew their deposits from London. The City had striven to shore up the Central European banks by generous, not to say rash, lending, and fruitlessly, too, for Austrian and German banks could not meet their obligations and repudiated their international liabilities by declaring a moratorium, thus freezing British banks' money in Germany. Meanwhile, their debt to foreign depositors amounted to sums variously estimated at between £250 million and £700 million. These depositors drew on the British gold reserves which were sucked away to Paris and New York. In short, as Skidelsky puts it, London was 'forced between 1929 and 1931, almost alone, to finance the world depression', attempting to maintain the gold standard as the foundation of the international financial system.

During July 1931, £33 million in gold and a further £33 million in foreign currency holdings were withdrawn from London. The flight from the pound became a Gadarene rush, and Britain urgently needed to borrow. Unfortunately potential lenders were convinced that Britain was drifting to bankruptcy because of reckless Government expenditure and loose administration. Abroad and at home the Government's policies were distrusted; the crisis had become political as well as economic.

MacDonald, leader of a minority Government, was in a fix. His Cabinet would not respond whole-heartedly to the need to slash Government expenditure, particularly if unemployment benefit were to come under the chopper. Whence then was help to come? It could only be from the Opposition. MacDonald appealed to the new Conservative Party Chairman, Lord Stonehaven, and floated the idea of an all-Party coalition. The message was passed to Baldwin and Baldwin rejected it. He had brought down one coalition and had no desire to participate in another. 'I will', Baldwin told Hankey, the Cabinet Secretary, on the last day of the session, 'do everything I can to help the Government in making economies, but I will not enter a Coalition Government.' Why should the Conservatives bail out Labour? Would Labour accept a tariff? No, they would not.

Baldwin was not unsympathetic to the Government's dilemma, and he got on well with MacDonald whom in tolerance, humanity and love of the countryside he resembled. But politics were politics, and so Baldwin set out for his usual holiday in Aix. He had got only as far as Angers when Davidson telephoned: the Government was breaking up, Baldwin must return. Unwillingly, he retraced his steps, arriving back in London early on the morning of 13 August 1931. In the afternoon he saw the austere, crippled Philip Snowden, Chancellor of the Exchequer, a man devoted to Free Trade and balancing his budget. Snowden told him that the Cabinet Economy Committee had agreed that each department should put forward its proposal for economies; Baldwin still would not be drawn into a political combination to do so. But he did privately tell Chamberlain: 'As the situation develops I may or may not have to take part in it, but that time hasn't arrived.' Whereupon he deposited the affair in Chamberlain's lap and returned to Aix.

He did not, however, forget all about the crisis as he walked through the upland woods and meadows. He studied the alarming report of the all-party Economic Committee chaired by the insurance magnate Sir George May. This forecast a £120m. budget deficit (it came to be £170m. in fact) and proposed saving £67m. from the unemployment insurance scheme and by cutting public service salaries. Baldwin also had a letter from Sir Robert Horne, whose personal character he sniffed at but whose financial sagacity he respected. A tariff was essential, wrote Horne. Revenue must be raised indirectly 'because the direct taxpayer is already burdened beyond bearing . . . We have since 1925 been trying to keep the pound sterling at twenty shillings when in fact it was not worth twenty shillings. This in itself was sufficient to produce an adverse balance of trade . . . The fact that we have to obtain credits from France and from America means that the pound is not worth its parity in francs or dollars, and I regret to tell you that the outflow continues to an alarming extent.' He did not think that MacDonald dared to do what needed to be done: 'I can easily envisage Ramsay as the buckram betrayer of our fortunes.'

Baldwin still made no move. As he explained in a letter to Chamberlain, the Government should 'get a lot of the dirt cleared up before we come in. To have the consequences of their finance exposed – and acknowledged to the world – within four months of their budget will be a wonderful lesson'. A little more stick was still required. Then, during the evening of 20 August the telephone tinkled in the Hôtel Bernascon at Aix. It was Chamberlain telling him that MacDonald's resignation seemed imminent, and urging him to return. En route for London he was met in Paris by Davidson, who put him in the picture. At Victoria station, where he arrived at 7.30 on Saturday evening, 22 August, batteries of press cameras and cheering crowds greeted him. He had come home, they thought, to save the country.

Baldwin soon found out that the whole Cabinet had provisionally agreed to cuts in Government expenditure of £56m., including £22m. from unemployment relief, limitation of benefit to twenty-six weeks, and after that a means test for transitional benefit. Beyond that some nine of the Cabinet of twenty would not go. The TUC General Council condemned all unemployment-pay cuts. Snowden knew that the cuts were not sufficient; Baldwin and Samuel (standing in for Lloyd George, who was ill) insisted that some £25m. more reduction was needed, amounting in all to over £80m. Only such a sum would enable credits to be negotiated; if not, a moratorium would have to be declared in a matter of days and, as Baldwin put it, the exchanges would go bust and there would be a run on the banks.

On Sunday morning, 23 August, the distraught MacDonald went to consult the King. Before anything drastic was done, the King proposed to see the two Opposition leaders. Baldwin could not be found – he was in fact somewhere chatting with Dawson, editor of *The Times* – and so Samuel was seen first. Samuel said that the 'best solution' would be for MacDonald to carry on, and impose the necessary measures. If he could not, the three parties should join in a National Emergency Government, preferably led by MacDonald. The King thought the latter was a good idea and when finally in the afternoon Baldwin turned up at the palace he was asked whether he would serve in a National Government under MacDonald. Baldwin said yes, which pleased the King: he was after all sinking 'party interests for the sake of the country'.

Baldwin went further; if MacDonald insisted on resigning he would form a Government himself if assured of Liberal support.

Baldwin *was* sinking party or at any rate personal differences since the idea of a Coalition with the Liberals was distasteful. Moreover he was not eager to return to office at all. He did not like Chamberlain's lip-smacking desire to detach MacDonald and a few others from the Labour Party and so split it irrevocably. That party he had long cossetted as the natural Opposition; he did not want to see it destroyed, but destroyed it was about to be.

That Sunday evening, 23 August, after an acrimonious Cabinet meeting, MacDonald told Baldwin that he would resign and had no intention of heading or even taking part in a Coalition. Baldwin left thinking that he would be required to form a Government. Next morning when the three party leaders met at the palace, the King appealed to MacDonald, and whoever of his Ministers would support him, to remain and help form a National Government. By sticking at his post, the King said, the Prime Minister's 'reputation would be much more enhanced than if he surrendered the Government of the country at such a crisis'. MacDonald agreed and Baldwin and Samuel again said they would serve under him. At the last Labour Cabinet meeting that evening, MacDonald, according to Sidney Webb, told his colleagues that 'he knew the cost, but could not refuse the King's request; that he would doubtless be renounced and ostracized, but could do no other'. Soon he was to be expelled from the Labour Party he had done so much to nurture. 'Deserted by some of his leading colleagues and by his party', wrote Baldwin to his wife, MacDonald did what he believed was best for the credit of the country.

The Cabinet was to be small. Baldwin became Lord President of the Council, a post that can be everything or nothing. Chamberlain, Hoare and Cunliffe-Lister joined him. From Labour, Snowden, Thomas and Lord Sankey remained and the Cabinet was completed by the two Liberals, Samuel and Reading. 'I am glad', wrote Beatrice Webb, 'that the other three (MacDonald, Snowden, Thomas) will disappear from the Labour world – they were rotten stuff.' Baldwin sharply defined the rôle of the new Government in a statement on 24 August: 'The National Government had been allotted a definite task, and on its completion it is understood that Parliament should be dissolved as soon as circumstances permit, and that each of the parties should be left free to place its policy before the electors for their approval. By this means no party will be called upon to sacrifice any of the principles in which it believes.'

MacDonald, broadcasting the following evening, explained that

commerce and well-being, not only of the British nation but of a large part of the civilized world, have been built up and rest upon the confidence in the pound sterling, and if that confidence be destroyed it means a dislocation of world trade from which everyone, and most of all the working people of this country, will suffer ... Everyone from whom we have borrowed, or who has placed deposits in our keeping, must be assured that the budget will be balanced, and that assurance is to be given at once, not only as a declaration of intention but as a programme with essential details.

MacDonald was, as he expected, 'ostracized' by such former colleagues as Henderson, Lansbury, Clynes and Greenwood. But nor was every Tory happy about Baldwin's joining MacDonald. Amery thought: 'So the old gangs have coalesced after all, and under the most futile of the old gangsters.' Austen Chamberlain, never exactly a lover of Baldwin, wrote: 'It really is hard lines that after being led for these last two years by a man unhelpful and inert as S.B., Neville should now be driven to exclaim to me that Ramsay is "infinitely worse".'

The Cabinet set to work and Baldwin went into almost continuous session, drafting legislation for the National Economy Bill. Snowden balanced his budget on 7 September. To meet the anticipated deficit of £170 million, he pushed up taxes, including income tax to five shillings in the pound. National debt redemption was suspended. Cuts of 10 per cent were made in the unemployment dole, and in all salaries paid by the State from Cabinet Ministers and judges to civil servants, teachers, the police and the armed forces – Baldwin gave himself a heftier cut, from £5,000 to £2,000 in salary. Owing to misunderstanding the naval economies caused a so-called naval mutiny at Invergordon and wild alarm among foreign holders of sterling, who thought it heralded the long awaited 'English revolution'.

Credits of £80m. had duly arrived and by 19 September were exhausted, the Bank losing £43m. in gold in one week. No further credits being forthcoming the gold standard was suspended, and with it the Act of 1925, by which Baldwin and Churchill had revived it. The suspension, which became in due course abolition, was exactly what the National Government had been formed to prevent. Meanwhile Baldwin unwillingly became father confessor to MacDonald, whose courage was ebbing away under the daily malevolence of his party towards him. He sent a revealing letter to Baldwin on 5 September 1931:

> I am a little unhappy about the future . . . Your party will support us but only for a comparatively brief time . . . The Liberals are in the land of the Absolutely Unknown. I have not left my party [he was expelled] and have no intention of doing so, but if it were to have a majority or could even form a Government after the next election, the country would again be faced with a financial crisis which would then in all probability break upon it and ruin it. My great weakness is that I have no machine and no newspaper with Labour principles behind it. Purely personal influences tends to evaporate when a fight comes, so that I do not suppose that I can be of great assistance to anybody . . . I would like you not to show this letter to even your most confidential friends – at any rate, without getting my sanction, as these things had better at the moment be kept to ourselves.

If there were to be a General Election, where indeed would MacDonald be? On 2 October he sent Baldwin another letter, pathetic and meandering, written in bed at 4.30 am in pencil:

> We are in a dreadful mix-up and unless we can get out of it disgrace is to be ours. The best way to escape from an entanglement is to see how we got into it. I have done what I have done to try and save this country from a financial crisis. That could not be and I go on to try and re-establish the position . . . Expansion of exports . . . Control of imports may be necessary and we must have power to deal with them . . . Who is the 'we' seeking power? The united Cabinet for a majority of the new House will be Conservative in all likelihood . . . Must we then be able to show national unity only by becoming parties to an election which in fact means that if we say we are not cutting tariffs out we are consenting to their being introduced whether we like it or not? That is the dilemma . . . It is too much to ask us to do that without some guarantee that we are not to appear after the election as the biggest boobies of our time . . . For us to have to resign before the New Year and leave a Conservative majority in power for five years would cover us with much ridicule . . . This is the root of the whole matter. So the Conservatives expect us to accept a formula which if the appeal to the country is successful leaves them at liberty within a week to disagree with us, turn us out and proceed to rule without us?

Next day, 3 October, the muddled MacDonald told the King that he 'was beginning to feel that he had failed and had better clear out'. The King, seeking to rally him, spoke severely: he must 'brace himself to tackle the present chaotic state of affairs'. The King succeeded. Yet MacDonald's dilemma, as a lifelong Socialist and one of the creators of his party, was real enough: 'He does not like the idea', wrote Wigram, the King's Secretary, 'of smashing up the Labour Party as the head of a Conservative organization.' But this he now did.

Baldwin agreed that the Coalition should go to the country as the National Government. Each candidate from the Conservative-Labour-Liberal 'cooperation of individuals', with their divergent views on tariffs, Free Trade and other questions, would be free to put his own viewpoint, but a Minister must not oppose another Minister's policy. The National Government would seek a 'doctor's mandate' to apply whatever remedy they could agree on to cure the country's ills. In MacDonald's *Appeal to the Nation* it was made clear that among the remedies to be considered would be 'tariffs, expansion of exports and restriction of imports, commercial treaties and mutual economic arrangements with the Dominions'. What MacDonald said should be considered with an open mind, Baldwin treated as essential, especially the tariff. For the rest, he agreed that the Government would be 'comprehensively national, and not sectional, in the obligations which it is to keep before it'; yet there must be no loss of political identity, because the immediate tasks were temporary.

Polling day was to be 27 October 1931, and electioneering was bitter, Snowden in particular abusing his former party as 'the party that ran away', and predicting that a Labour victory would be 'Bolshevism run mad'. The results of the election were not just a landslide, they were an earthquake. National Government supporters took 556 of the 615 seats, the bulk being Conservative (471); Opposition candidates won only 56 seats, Labour being reduced to 46; all Labour's former front bench were defeated except the pacifist George Lansbury, who thereby became leader of the Opposition. A victory that spoke volumes was that of the man these losers had so bitchily blackguarded; MacDonald, with only a rudimentary organization, held Seaham Harbour, one of the solidest and leftist Labour constituencies in the country, by 5,951.

On the whole breath-taking affair, Davidson commented: 'The British nation has done through the ballot-box what Continental countries can only do by revolution. We have a dictatorship and the Conservative Party has sufficient members of Parliament to give it a majority over everyone else . . .' While everyone (except the defeated) hailed the almost certainly never-to-be-repeated result, Baldwin took it calmly: 'The country has sent out an S.O.S. to the Government and now we have to rise to it,' was his first reaction. He insisted that it was 'no party victory'; it proved that the British people were for national cooperation and against 'the propaganda of the demagogue' and 'the insidious doctrines of class warfare'. Yet in votes cast the National Government was endorsed by not much more than two to one, something over fourteen million in favour to rather under seven million against. Even so it was obvious that, as Snowden said, 'millions of unemployed and former Labour voters have put national interests before party'.

Cabinet-making caused some hard bargaining between Baldwin, MacDonald and Samuel but it was eventually agreed that Conservatives were to have eleven out of the twenty seats, which by no means represented their strength in the Commons; the Simonite and Samuelite Liberals got five places, which was more than they deserved, and MacDonald's own National Labour followers got four. Baldwin settled, as before, for the Lord Presidency, plus the use of 11 Downing Street, for which, he told the King, he 'was very grateful, as he was very badly-off now and a house with no rent and taxes would be a godsend'. Chamberlain took the Exchequer, Snowden went to the Lords, though remaining Lord Privy Seal. Simon was Foreign Secretary, his Liberal opponent Samuel Home Secretary. The three fighting posts – which at that time seemed of little consequence – were filled by Hailsham (War), Londonderry (Air) and the former Chief Whip, Eyres-Monsell (Admiralty).

In this motley Cabinet Baldwin had the greatest prestige, MacDonald little; he led by far the biggest party in Parliament, MacDonald a small rump. Was not MacDonald, therefore, his puppet? A positive answer must be qualified. He never encroached on MacDonald's privilege as Prime Minister; he seldom initiated a proposal in Cabinet, though, as Samuel wrote, 'when a discussion was taking an awkward turn, he would intervene at the end with some brief observation, full of common sense, that helped us to an agreement'. Nevertheless, he was *not* Prime Minister, so that criticisms levelled against him during this period must be levelled against MacDonald, and the Cabinet as a whole. The arrangement suited Baldwin, as Tom Jones reports in his diary: 'This being second and not first suits him (Baldwin) perfectly and frees him from final decisions and therefore from worry.' Yet it was Baldwin who held the Coalition together; he was seated, as someone wrote, 'at the exact centre of a nicely balanced seesaw'.

Baldwin did not always find his balancing act easy. Seeking to moderate, he sometimes found himself acting as a brake, other times as the accelerator. It was he who, for example, eased past the diehard clamour the Statute of Westminster in November 1931, which recognized that the Empire of the Dominions had grown up and that all that bound them together was common allegiance to the Crown, and sentiment. His general attitude was nicely put by the Marxist John Strachey in the summer of 1932. Baldwin, he wrote in *The Coming Struggle for Power*, 'realizes instinctively that almost anything that anyone *does* will only make matters worse. He is the perfect statesman for an empire in decline; he is forever stopping things. He, in effect, attempts to stop the decline, and if he does not wholly deceive himself into believing that he can do that, he can at any rate, he knows, prevent it being immeasurably accelerated by the foolish actions of others.'

The Government pressed the general tariff through in February 1932 by 454 votes to 32 Liberals and 46 Labour. The Liberals in the Government were allowed a strange 'agreement to differ', not unlike that given by Wilson to his Government during the Common Market referendum debate in 1975. Baldwin, summing up the debate, said the tariff would cheapen British production by enabling industry to run full time. Iron, steel and other hard-hit industries could, under the shelter of a tariff, carry out reorganization that could attract capital, thus enabling new plant to be laid down. Unemployment would then fall. Behind the dangling carrot was a hint of the stick; industries which were incompetent or did not 'rationalize' might find their tariff withdrawn.

Along with tariffs came an active monetary policy; an example is the Exchange Equalization Account. Interventionism had arrived and was being practised. Baldwin observed: 'There is no question that the State could do much to provide favourable conditions and that all parties were committed to a degree of intervention in the life of the individual that would have seemed excessive or tyrannical to Bentham.' But, he claimed, individual freedom and enterprise had been preserved. By March 1932 Baldwin thought the Government's policies were working: 'Six months ago we felt the greatest anxiety about the stability of our currency. Today people are looking to sterling in many parts of the world as the one safe and natural anchorage.'

Baldwin often stood in for MacDonald, who suffered eye strain and bouts of extreme fatigue. Once, 'feeling very tired', MacDonald told Baldwin that he would never fight another election. He would retire with the close of the present Parliament. 'I', Baldwin told Tom Jones, 'feel very much the same. I must carry on for this Parliament and use what prestige I have got to keep our fellows together.' MacDonald remained very sensitive about his position, complaining to Baldwin on 3 December 1931 that Lord Stonehaven, Chairman of the Tory Party, had said: 'We have a National Government with a mandate to carry out Tory policy.' MacDonald went on: 'If he is right, then some of us have grossly misled millions of electors and we cannot possibly remain under that imputation . . . We have all been so distracted by day to day troubles . . . have had to live from agitation to agitation.' Stonehaven replied that it was all an attempt by the *News Chronicle* to make mischief; but his alleged statement was, of course, true.

Baldwin passed some hot and sticky days in Ottawa in July–August 1932, leading the British delegation to the Empire Economic Union talks. He saw the Dominions' and Britain's choice as limited either to lowering barriers between themselves, which he preferred, or raising them against others. R. B. Bennett, the Canadian Prime Minister, said to have the manners of a Chicago policeman and the temperament of a Hollywood film star, was out for his own country's interests and for import quotas operated against foreigners; so were New Zealand and Australia. In the upshot, individual rather than general agreements were made; 80 per cent of Empire products were to continue to have free entrance into the British markets and tariffs were put on foreign imports of wheat. Britain promised to keep her 10 per cent import duty on goods. The Dominions in return would increase preference in Britain's favour.

Baldwin did not think much of the Ottawa decisions because they in no way helped towards what he in these years began to think of as an ideal to be aimed at, namely Free Trade within larger world units of which the Empire was to be the first. Amery saw with some dismay that Baldwin was drifting from the Ark of the Covenant: he 'seemed to regard a tariff as more in the nature of a necessary evil in a wicked world than as the natural and normal economic expression of national policy'. Baldwin wanted to use British tariffs to clear the way for world Free Trade. The formation of regional *blocs* would be a first step towards such *blocs* as the European Economic Community.

The Ottawa agreements were too much for the Liberals, who resigned from the Goverment: 'the dirty dogs – they always behave like this when rough weather approaches,' observed Baldwin. He thought he saw the hand of Lloyd George, for 'the Goat' was back from his illness looking 'very wicked and very well'. MacDonald believed that the Government was breaking up and that he would have to resign. Baldwin would have none of it: 'I told Ramsay when the National Government was formed that if they tried to hound him out unfairly, they could boot me out too.' To MacDonald he wrote: 'Don't worry. You are bound to carry on.' He saw that the defection of the Liberals was an irrelevance, and MacDonald stayed on.

Dealing with defence matters is like 'walking in a bog', said Sir Maurice Hankey in 1932, and as Secretary to the Cabinet and to the Committee of Imperial Defence, with his finger in the pie of half a dozen sub-committees, he knew. Into this bog stepped Baldwin, replacing the frequently absent Prime Minister. The Lord President was uniquely well equipped to take his place; he had long sat on the C.I.D. and had usually been its chairman; he had chaired the C.I.D. and Cabinet committees related to defence, he was in close contact with the Chiefs of Staff whose committee he had set up, with scientists and other experts. When the C.I.D. proposed action to the Cabinet there he was again to put his prestige behind proposals he himself had often drafted. In transmitting decisions to Parliament and the public, he became in effect the Cabinet's spokesman on defence.

Neither Baldwin nor any other senior Minister had much time to think about war during the hubbub caused by crisis and coalition in 1931. Then a flash of lightning shot across the Far Eastern skies: the Japanese army invaded Manchuria, officially part of China whose writ, however, did not in practice run there, and after an 'incident' was soon swirling round the outskirts of Shanghai, the International Settlement for whose defence Britain was in part responsible and where some £200m. of British money was invested.

This Oriental coruscation gave Baldwin, chairing the Cabinet's Far Eastern Committee, a 'nightmare': he visualized the Far East, where from Hong Kong to Borneo Britain had vast economic interests, in flames and he knew that Britian had too small a fire brigade to put them out. Churchill and the Labour Government had done their work only too well; for instance, Britain's Air Force came fifth in the world league in 1931. What about America? As usual America would talk and do nothing and would not let Britain do anything either; such was the real meaning of the London Naval Treaty that had been signed by the Labour Government in 1930, 'parity for America at the expense of Britain', as Bridgeman had said. In such circumstances to talk of sanctions imposed by the League was merely absurd.

Baldwin summed up the situation to Tom Jones:

I think I see the position quite clearly. With Russia and America out of the League, sanctions are a mistake. I've always thought so. You can't enforce them against a first-class power. The very people like Bob Cecil who have made us disarm, and quite right too, are now urging us forward to take action. But where will action lead us to? If we withdraw ambassadors, that's only the first step. What's the next? If you enforce an economic boycott you'll have war declared by Japan and she will seize Singapore and Hong Kong and we can't, as we are placed, stop her. You'll get nothing out of Washington but words, big words, but only words. That's what I told Van (sittart) this morning. We can't be going along one road, outside the League, with America, and also at the same time profess loyalty to the League and its procedure.

Baldwin was appalled by Britain's military impotence that the Japanese aggression revealed to him, and it was not going to be easy to cure it. Even during the urgent talks in Cabinet while Shanghai was being bombed and beleaguered, Chamberlain, the Chancellor, had broken in like a housemaster upon misbehaving boys to say; 'The fact is that in the present circumstances we are no more in a position financially and economically to engage in a major war in the Far East than we are militarily . . . The Treasury submits that at the present time financial risks are greater than any other that we can estimate.' Perhaps they were. All the same Baldwin threw his weight behind the Services' demand for cancellation of the Ten Year Rule and for an immediate start on repairing the Far Eastern defences. The Cabinet agreed but with the stifling proviso that total expenditure should not be increased without taking into account the state of the economy.

In any case it seemed almost indelicate to talk of rearmament while the grand Disarmament Conference was lumbering on in Geneva. Baldwin never had much hope of it though as chairman of the Disarmament Committee of the Cabinet he went through the motions, even blessing an unworkable scheme to abolish naval and military aircraft. It was all nonsense, of course; Britain had already disarmed to danger point, and Baldwin said publicly on 9 November 1932: 'The time has come to an end when Great Britain can proceed with unilateral disarmament.'

The Germans, too, under Prime Minister Von Papen, were demanding 'equality of rights' (*Gleichberechtigung*), had left the Disarmament Conference, were training youths under military officers, welding irregular forces into a militia, and laying down a pocket battleship (later known as the 'Admiral Graf Spee'). It was, thought Hankey, 'the penultimate stage' before full and open rearmament in blatant disregard of Versailles. Baldwin was also told in the C.I.D. of the ghastly effects of bombing, and had been greatly distressed.

Now in turn he distressed and alarmed the public, and on 10 November 1932 caused a sensation in the House of Commons. After developing the proposition that while disarmament by itself would not stop war it would reduce the dangers of making war, he added three short, sharp sentences: 'I think it is as well for the man in the street to realize that there is no power on earth that can protect him from being bombed. Whatever people may tell him, the bomber will always get through. The only defence is in offence, which means that you have to kill more women and children more quickly than the enemy if you want to save yourselves.'

This was shocking stuff for the breakfast table. Yet it was all too true: the bombers would always get through, as was demonstrated clearly in the air exercises in 1934 when only two out of five bombers were intercepted, and in London, as one observer jocularly remarked, 'neither the Air Ministry nor the Houses of Parliament should bother us any more'. Even after radar was developed, the bombers still got through, as London and other cities were to realize, though, being routed by Fighter Command, they had no decisive effect on the outcome of the war.

Baldwin's speech upset Churchill. There was, he thought, a

sense of fatalism and helplessness about it. Perhaps he was thinking of Baldwin's further remarks, about the uselessness and impracticability of the limitations of armaments tediously bandied about at Geneva, or more particularly Baldwin's mysterious peroration. If the conscience of the 'young men' came to regard the bomber as evil and should go, 'the thing will be done', he said. If they did not feel like that, 'when the next war comes and European civilization is wiped out, as it will be, and by no force more than that force, then do not let them lay the blame on the old men. Let them remember that they, principally, or they alone, are responsible for the terrors that have fallen upon the earth.'

This revealed more of Baldwin's overwrought nerves than of his ratiocinative powers. Could he really be appealing to what he had called the 'scorched and cynical generation' to vote out of power any Government that built bombers? In that case it would be unilateral disarmament with a vengeance such as the Socialists preached; and with what hope of success was he asking the young men of France, Italy, Russia and America to do the same?

There was a smell of pacifism about the speech, as Churchill had detected. Baldwin dreaded war. Even a war purely for defence was felt to be intrinsically and inescapably horrible, and Baldwin was expressing the thoughts of an overwhelming majority of his fellow-countrymen when he said that war was 'the most fearful terror and prostitution of men's knowledge . . . whoever starts it knows that he is condemning to death and mutilation and possibly starvation as many civilians, men, women and children, as may be killed in the fighting Services. More of the great works of man, works that distinguish him from the beasts, may be destroyed in four years of intensive bombing than the Goths, Huns and Vandals could accomplish in a century. It is enough to make Attila turn in his grave with envy . . . That is not a prompting of physical fears: it is fear for the minds and souls of our fellow men.' Prof. Bernard Brodie was to write: 'In the treatise on strategy, battlefields seldom have the smell of death.' To Baldwin they always did, and when he had to receive – and, worse, take decisions on – the reports of the C.I.D. and the Chiefs of Staff, the smell of death must often have been in his nostrils, and in his mind's eye a glimpse of the absurdity of nations building battleships for other nations to sink in the middle of the ocean.

But where did horror of war end, and defeatism begin? George

Lansbury, leader of the Opposition, was openly defeatist: 'I would close every recruiting station, disband the Army, and disarm the Air Force. I would abolish the whole dreadful equipment of war and say to the world "Do your worst".' Baldwin might shudder at the thought of war but he never forgot that the prime duty of any Government is to make sure of its country's security, even when the official Opposition puts every obstacle in its path, even when it begins to appear, as in 1933 it did, that the country supports a pacifist Opposition. The Conservatives lost a series of by-elections in that year, notably at East Fulham in October 1933, where a Conservative majority of 14,000 was turned into a Labour majority of 5,000. It is clear now that rearmament was not the only issue at East Fulham; housing, the means test, food prices and employment were as important. Nevertheless, after huge swings against the Government at Kilmarnock, Rusholme, Harborough and Cambridge, it was obvious that if there were to be a General Election Labour would win by at least a hundred seats. Then, as Baldwin told Vansittart, 'you will have the Socialists, who will give you no rearmament at all, instead of me who gives you not enough'. Logically, therefore, the National Government must hang on, save the peace if it could, prepare for war if it could not.

Baldwin's faint hope that something would emerge from the Disarmament Conference faded after he visited it during his Aix holiday in 1933. France would not allow Germany to equalize up nor would she equalize down; the talk bogged down in wrangles about samples, calibres, prototypes, defensive or offensive weapons. 'We paddled in a purée of words and hoped to catch a formula,' said Vansittart. Baldwin returned to Aix. 'Walking alone among these hills', he wrote to Tom Jones, 'I have come to the conclusion the world is stark mad. I have no idea what is the matter with it but it's all wrong and at times I am sick to death of being an asylum attendant. I think we are the sanest but the disease is catching . . . I leave a little part of me behind walking, walking in the hills,' he said on leaving.

At the beginning of that year, 1933, Adolf Hitler had become Chancellor of a Germany with seven million unemployed, little foreign trade and no gold reserves. His advent to power, by tricky but still constitutional paths, caused little comment abroad; he had been ranting about the place for quite a long time, and was not expected to last long. In England the Liberal *News Chronicle* thought his appointment 'a good and necessary thing'. But before long, news of Hitler's treatment of Jews and pacifists, of his warlike attitudes (though not towards Britain), and his abrupt departure from the League of Nations made some people sit up and take notice.

Baldwin began official and unofficial enquiries about the personality of Hitler, which fascinated him. He met Ribbentrop, Hitler's emissary, at lunch in London in November 1933, and was invited to visit Germany, but did not. Eden met Hitler and found him reasonable, willing to hold to the Locarno pact though having no regard for Versailles. Even Churchill at this time wrote of Hitler: 'I admire men who stand up for their country after defeat.' But valid information, rather than speculation, about Hitler and his intentions was hard to come by, for he put up an immense smokescreen of bluff and lies. As for *Mein Kampf*, its threatening foreign policy chapters had been written nearly a decade earlier by a man dreaming of power but far from it. British military planners still thought of Japan as the strongest and likeliest enemy.

Yet Baldwin, defending the Air Estimates in the Commons on 8 March 1934, said that 'if all our efforts for an agreement fail, and if it is not possible to obtain equality in such matters as I have indicated, then any Government of this country – a National Government more than any and *this* Government – will see to it that in air strength and air power this country shall no longer be in a position inferior to any country within striking distance of our shore'. The latter phrase pointed not to Japan but at Europe. As yet, however, Hitler's policy was cautious; he needed to establish himself more firmly at home; Germany was isolated and still militarily weak.

A few months later Baldwin was still not certain, he told the *Manchester Guardian* editor W. P. Crozier on 12 June 1934, whether Germany meant peace or war. Certainly, he did not believe in war in the near future, though most of the people who talked to him took a gloomy view about Germany's ultimate intention. At all events, he held that the Government could not take risks; the country had to have adequate means of defence 'so far as those could be provided', and in the censure debate of 30 July 1934, following the announcement of increases in the RAF, he issued a warning directly to Germany and Britain: 'The greatest crime to our own people is to be afraid to tell the truth. The old frontiers are gone; when you think of the defence of England you no longer think of the chalk cliffs of Dover; you think of the Rhine. That is where our frontier lies . . .'

What the Government proposed was little enough and that little had been slashed in Cabinet by Chamberlain 'in the light of politics and finance' from £76m. to £50m. The RAF would increase by 41½ squadrons – about 820 aircraft – over the next five years. Even so Attlee, speaking for the Opposition, said: 'We deny the need for increased air armaments. We deny the proposition that an increased RAF will make for the peace of the world and we reject altogether the claim to parity.' But what of the Army and the Navy? Baldwin wanted them strengthened, too: a decision was taken to spend the maximum amount over four years that the Chancellor would countenance. But in the end naval increases were sacrificed for the politically desirable restoration of the cuts made in the 1931 crisis in salaries and pay. There had to be some butter, not all guns.

By now Hitler had left the League of Nations, and his Nazi party murdered a section of its own leadership. Hitler himself was one of the killers: Röhm, who had created the thug S.A. organization, General Schleicher, Gregor Strasser, and a host of others, some quite accidentally involved, were slaughtered in the most gruesome circumstances. 'I have the impression', wrote Ambassador Rumbold with a fine irony, 'that the persons directing the Hitler Government are not normal.' Local Austrian Nazis staged a coup which, though they killed the Chancellor Dollfus, failed and was therefore disavowed by Hitler.

What about the possibility of a coup in Britain itself? Baldwin, as Lord President, was alert to the disorders being nightly created by clashes mainly between Mosley's British Union of Fascists, wearing their black shirts, and groups of Leftists; and in July 1934 he asked the Home Office for a note on the various 'shirt' organizations. The B.U.F. were clearly the best funded and were spending at a rate of £8,255 a week, but there were other strange and mad organizations, though no madder than Hitler's gangs in the 1920s. The Blue Shirts had been founded by Cmdr. O. Locker-Lampson in 1932 to combat Communism; the Green Shirts, professing Maj. Douglas's Social Credit theories; the Red Shirts, the I.L.P.'s Guild of Youth; the Brown Shirts of the British Fascists' Association. Baldwin's curiosity resulted two years later in the Public Order Act, banning political uniforms. If people 'in great numbers' became adherents of either Communism or Fascism, there could be only one end to it – civil war – he said in a broadcast to schools on 6 March 1934.

Baldwin had hoped that the increase in air armament he had announced would have pulled Hitler up short, but it did not seem to have done so. Alarming reports were current of German expansion, hints of mechanized divisions forming and munitions factories ready for intensive output. Great increases were forecast in air armament, and Churchill gave such forecasts currency in the Commons. Baldwin replied that he believed Churchill's figures were exaggerated. The trouble was that 'the state of apprehension that exists throughout Europe has been largely caused by a want of knowledge of what was going on inside Germany'. Baldwin claimed that if Germany continued to expand her programme 'without acceleration', Britain would still in one year's time be 50 per cent stronger. His claim is supported by post-war inquiry; German war production expanded with far less speed than some of the Intelligence agencies were claiming.

All the same, the Cabinet could not ignore the information that it was receiving, and on 4 March 1935 it issued a further White Paper on Defence. Baldwin called it a declaration that Britain must be strong enough 'to repel an aggressor or to fulfil obligations'. It was mild enough, making no mention of any expeditionary force being planned, although there was a hint of Civil Defence measures, and after referring to arms increases announced by Germany, Japan, Russia and the USA, it quietly observed that 'an additional expenditure on the armaments of the three Defence Services can, therefore, no longer be safely postponed'.

Temperate as the Defence White Paper was, Hitler reacted abruptly. On 9 March 1935 Goering revealed the existence of the Luftwaffe; on 16 March Hitler announced the introduction of conscription, saying that Germany needed a land army of thirty-six divisions, some half a million men. (Perhaps this was a reply to France's doubling her conscription period from one year to two.) In the same month Hitler told Simon and Eden in Berlin that Germany had already reached parity with Britain in the air and intended to do so with France. It was untrue, but it caused great alarm in the Cabinet. Baldwin accepted the figures; in so doing he believed that he should apologize for misleading the House when the year before he had said that Britain would still be 50 per cent ahead of Germany in air armaments. But he had added, 'if German expansion did not accelerate'. Now it had, or appeared to have done so. Baldwin's apology on 22 May 1935, though warmly cheered in the House, was unnecessary; he could well have defended his earlier statement. He did not, perhaps hoping to divert Opposition attention from the fact that he was also announcing that air rearmament was being accelerated.

Hitler's threatening posture caused a flurry of pact-making: the Stresa 'front' in April 1935, between Britain, France and Italy, which declared the three countries' opposition to unilateral repudiation of peace treaties, and reaffirmed the necessity to maintain Austrian independence and to build up Eastern European security; the Franco-Soviet non-aggression pact; and one in which Baldwin was deputed by MacDonald as chief negotiator, namely the Anglo-German naval agreement. It was the only one of the three which worked, but it was an odd business. It limited German naval expansion to 35 per cent of that of Britain's fleet, and Hitler adhered to it until the spring of 1939. Thus, as Baldwin hoped, it avoided an arms race with Germany in the naval sphere at a time when Japan showed signs of renewing her war against China, which in turn faced Britain with the possibility of having to fight a naval war on two fronts. The agreement neutralized one front. Baldwin saw also that he could present it to the electorate as a success in arms limitation. But to his colleagues he said: 'It may well be that we are on a road leading to war. If so, then the agreement is tantamount to erecting a danger sign on the road ahead.' Baldwin meant that, since massive naval construction could not take place in secret, the world would swiftly hear of it and draw its conclusions as to Hitler's real intentions. The agreement, in short, was a litmus paper. But it publicly put finis to Versailles and evoked cries from France of 'perfide Albion'.

Baldwin, active as he was in defence matters and foreign affairs, spent as much if not more effort on pressing through his India Bill, and it became law in 1935. 'Pressing through' meant, principally, countering the near-frenzied opposition of Churchill, who threatened to smash the Government: 'I did not mean to be smashed,' Baldwin coolly remarked. Nor was he. On 7 June 1935 he succeeded the battered and bewildered MacDonald as Prime Minister, MacDonald taking Baldwin's place as Lord President.

'It was tragic', Baldwin remembered, 'to see him in his closing days as Prime Minister, losing the thread of his speech and turning to ask a colleague why people were laughing.' Poor 'Ramshackle Mac', as such erstwhile friends as Lady Londonderry dubbed him now! So confused was he that he thought Baldwin was not to succeed him but to serve with him under Neville Chamberlain.

Baldwin took the opportunity to make some changes in this, his last, Ministry. Hoare replaced Simon as Foreign Secretary, Simon in Eden's words having 'too penetrating a discernment and too frail a conviction'; Eden himself entered the Cabinet as Minister for League of Nations Affairs. Cunliffe-Lister took Londonderry's place as Air Minister. It seems Baldwin would have liked to bring back Churchill but was overborne by the majority of Tories: Churchill had dished himself by his intemperance over India. Baldwin, however, in one of his flashes of divination, wrote to Davidson: 'As for Winston I feel we should not give him a post at this stage. Anything he undertakes he puts his heart and soul into. If there is going to be a war – and no one can say there is not – we must keep him fresh to be our War Prime Minister.'

Churchill himself seems to have borne no grudge about his exclusion from the Cabinet, for later in the year, 1935, he wrote to Baldwin: 'Things are in such a state that it is a blessing to have at the head of affairs a man who people will rally round.' The two men made a sort of peace. Meeting in the gents at the Commons, Baldwin remarked: 'There's at least this platform we can appear on together'. Next month, July 1935, Churchill accepted Baldwin's offer – made against Neville Chamberlain's will – of a seat on the newly formed Air Research Committee. Baldwin agreed that, within the limits of security, this would not spike Churchill's critical guns.

Yet in the end it was Baldwin who got air rearmament really going. 'All of us at the Air Ministry', the new Minister Cunliffe-Lister wrote, 'who set out to achieve a revolutionary programme of expansion and innovation, the ordering of thousands of aircraft off the drawing-boards, the Shadow Factories, the integration of leading scientists with the air staff which gave us radar, could not have achieved what we did without Baldwin's support.' Baldwin in fact had comprehended the enormous advantages produced by the country's scientists in the form of the Rolls Royce Merlin engines, the variable pitch propeller, the automatic eight-gun turret, 'echo' (i.e. radar) and knew that figures of air strength in obsolescent aircraft had little significance.

Meanwhile, large sections of the public were in a muddled state of mind, as the 'Peace' ballot, whose result was declared on 28 June 1935, emphasized. Baldwin thought its questions were tendentious, but he could not ignore the fact that of the $11\frac{1}{2}$m. signatories only $6\frac{3}{4}$m. agreed that an aggressor should be stopped by war. Or, put another way, nearly five million people would not agree to war in any circumstances, and thereby rejected the Covenant of the League of Nations and Locarno. Ironically Italy, a member of the League of Nations and of the Locarno pact, was readying herself for a prime piece of aggression and on 3 October 1935 invaded Abyssinia. Her fellow League members branded her as an aggressor and convicted her of violating the Covenant.

A few days later Baldwin asked the King for a dissolution, and polling day was fixed for 14 November. It was shrewd timing since, as John Gunther pointed out, the election was in 'the midst of a grave international crisis when people were mentally bound to support a strong "safe" Government'. Baldwin exploited the crisis to press rearmament. He had said as recently as July that 'we are not satisfied with the defence of this country. We do not believe our defences are in that condition yet that will enable us to speak with the voice we should in favour of that collective security which is gradually commending itself to the people of this country'. Now, in October, under cover of the Abyssinian crisis, he got the Cabinet to sanction a plan for seven annual naval programmes costing £200 million, and, most important, it was agreed that financial consideration might have to give way to accelerated programmes for both army and navy. Fruition date would be 1939; but the plan's progress was to be determined by the ability of Germany, then borrowing £1,000 million a year for armaments, to start a war. It might be speeded up. But, obviously, not in time for action against Italy.

Baldwin, in calling an election, knew that the Abyssinian war and the demand for military sanctions in support of 'collective security' put the Labour Party in a jam: their leaders quarrelled, some – the majority – supporting military action against Italy, others pursuing the pacifist line, others again taking the Marxist attitude that every war entered upon by a capitalist government is an imperialist and capitalist war. So the Government could with justice accuse the Opposition of being at once pacifist and war-mongering.

Baldwin took full advantage of these divisions among his op-ponents. He opened his campaign with a brilliant speech in which, in Tom Jones's summary, he 'denounced the isolationists, and reconciled the party to the League by supporting rearmament, and reconciled the pacifists to rearmament by supporting the Covenant. Spoke strongly in favour of trade unions', who had come out firmly for restraining Italy even at the risk of war'. Domestically Baldwin had a good record to offer the electorate. Despite the stricken areas where unemployment had bitten and scarred and dole was scarcely adequate for existence, the number of insured persons unemployed was declining, production had risen and output per head was up by 20 per cent. The balance of payments and of trade were favourable. Housing boomed and slums steadily vanished; consumer and ser-vice industries grew steadily. Deflationary measures were modified and a cheap money policy began: the bank rate from 1932 was 2 per cent. The Government's moderate tariff policy seemed to have been painless if not obviously beneficial.

All the same, what Baldwin was really after in the 1935 election was a mandate from the electorate for spending more money on armaments. He began to want it as desperately as he had wanted the self-government for India Act. Privately, he told Neville Chamberlain that he believed the electorate would now accept re-armament if some such phrase as 'repairing the gaps in our defences' were used. Publicly he put his theme thus: Britain did not need huge forces, 'no great armaments', but modern ones – 'the best that can be obtained today'. Such defences would be the surest guarantee of world peace.

The Labour Party were not deceived. They knew that Baldwin wanted a big expansion of Britain's armed forces, and their election manifesto rejected it: 'The Government is a danger to the peace of the world, to the security of this country . . . Labour will propose to other nations the complete abolition of all the national Air Forces, the effective international control of civil aviation and the creation of an international agreement in the national manufacture of, and trade in, arms.' Despite all that, said Baldwin in a speech, ever anxious to keep the nation united, he believed the Labour Opposition still stood 'in their heart of hearts for our Constitution and for our free Parliament' (a sentiment for which Lansbury thanked him by letter). Nevertheless the intransigent statement had to be contradicted and Baldwin deployed all his eloquence in a speech on 1 October 1935, made ironically enough to the Peace Society:

'We live under the shadow of the last war and its memories still sicken us ... That swathe of death cut through the loveliest and best of our contemporaries; public life has suffered because those who would have been ready to take over from our tired and disillusioned generation are not there.' He conjured up this 'dear, dear land of ours ... the level evening sun over an English meadow, with the rooks tumbling noisily home into the elms, of the ploughman ...' Then, bang came the conclusion: 'Make no mistake; every piece of all the life that we have and hold and cherish is in jeopardy in this great issue.' The Socialist Harold Laski, long one of his admirers, was thrilled: 'The greatest speech a Prime Minister has ever made,' he said.

Baldwin, while stressing that 'not a penny more than was absolutely necessary' would be spent on defence, was careful to avoid personal attack on those who differed from him: had he done so he would have put at risk what Davidson called 'the industrial peace and cooperation which was there on the day when it was most required'. If, thought Davidson, 'Churchill and his friends had been in power, and made the speeches they did, they would have been swept out of office in the 1935 election'. As it was, Britain went into war in 1939 a united nation; for this, Baldwin's moderation over the years was in part responsible. In retrospect, all that really separated the rearming Baldwin and the rearming Churchill was the industrial basis.

Baldwin had made his point – more money for arms – and did not doubt that he would win. Tom Jones records: 'He is in capital form and quietly happy at the approaching elections and with far more faith in himself than in the old days.' His faith was justified when polling day came on 14 November 1935. Of the unique 1931 gain in seats by the National Government, only 80 were lost. Over 70 per cent of the electorate voted and the Government got 53.6 of that vote. Conservatives and allies won 432 seats, Labour 154 and the Samuelite Liberals 20. This time MacDonald lost for his seat, though another, Scottish Universities, was found him.

Baldwin had his mandate for rearmament. For him the 1935 election was a personal triumph, as Tom Jones noted:

He has made no mistakes. He timed the election correctly in his party's interest. Six months hence and it is certain the results would be less favourable to him. He has only very slowly and with obvious reluctance proclaimed the need for more armaments; he has avoided all trace of the *Daily Mail*'s lust to arm the nation to the teeth and has also kept clear of Winston's enthusiasm for ships and guns. He has strictly confined the extent to which he was prepared to move against Italy and distinguished Mussolini from the Italian people. Labour pacifists, on the other hand, have clamoured for closing the Suez Canal and for other bellicose sanctions. While rejecting L.G.'s swollen programme of public works he has announced a programme sufficiently expansive to give heart to those concerned for the unemployed. Over all he has thrown that halo of faith and hope, free from meretricious ornament, which inspires confidence.

Baldwin at sixty-eight was once more the triumphant leader of his party, but this mild-mannered man did not look the part. During an interview, the editor of the *Manchester Guardian*, W. P. Crozier, examined him closely:

I had never seen him before, and in his photographs his face had always seemed to be chiefly amiable and a little whimsical, just as his speeches sound simple, honest and ingenuous. Actually he is not like that at all. His face is rugged and knobbly; his right eye is either going wrong or has some sort of cast in it and was mostly half-shut. But the characteristic of his face is its determination and shrewdness – or rather, because it is much more than shrewdness, a sort of deep rustic craftiness ... Baldwin seemed to me to look shrewd and crafty in a rather grim and hard way. I got quite a new idea of him and for the first time understood how he had come to be leader of the Tory Party and Prime Minister. The good-natured mellow look of the photographs was only there when he greeted me and again when he said good-bye ...

The observer of Baldwin usually saw in him what they expected to see. It was natural for the scholarly author, Helen Waddell, to write: 'Not a bit like the stockbroker photographs but rather like a classical scholar turned farmer with a kind of innocence about him.' Harold Nicolson, National Labour MP, was an author, and accustomed to look for revealing quirks and oddities. 'There is something very strange about Stanley Baldwin. At first sight he is a solid English gentleman, but then one observes odd nervous tricks. He has an extraordinarily unpleasant habit of smelling at his notes and licking the edges slightly as if they were the flaps of an envelope. He scratches himself continuously. There are russet patches across his head and face. And a strange movement of the head, with half-closed eyes, like some tortoise half-awake smelling the air – blinking, snuffy, neurotic.'

Baldwin's little eccentricities did not decrease as he grew older. From his baggy pockets he would produce curious objects such as a box which, when turned over, mooed plaintively like a cow in labour. When R. A. Butler's dog nipped his leg, Baldwin promptly produced an iodine pencil from his pocket, as though prepared for every minor eventuality. These oddities were scarcely more significant than the watch-chain on his waistcoat. The reality was a man who had for many years exercised great power at the top of the political pile, and had set into a personality of dignity and presence. He enjoyed his position, liked the hushed reverential air which his appearance always evoked, liked being the chief figure on great occasions, or, when in procession as Chancellor of Cambridge, his trailing gown held up by a page.

As a speaker he became better and better. There he stood, looking ordinary, rather pale, slightly surprised at the acclamations, fidgeting with his notes. He talked plainly with few inflexions, now catching the lapels of his jacket and swinging them back to reveal his shirt sleeves, now smoothing his hair with both hands, occasionally plucking at the tip of his nose. Then his hands would go deep into his jacket pockets and one would come out to wag an emphasizing forefinger. The expression on his face changed constantly, though a humorous twinkle lingered in his eyes, the jaw square, the brow open. He neither tried for rhetorical effect nor poured out scintillating wit, yet his memorabilia were frequent: 'Dictatorship is like a giant beech tree – very magnificent to look at in its prime but nothing grows under it.' Or advising young people on the qualities needed in public life: 'Use your common sense, avoid logic, love your fellow-men, have a profound faith in your own people, grow the hide of a rhinoceros'; or 'To be a saint, or even a good citizen, it is not necessary to be a great mathematician. There are simple truths which seem hidden from the high and mighty and revealed to farm labourers and charwomen.'

He particularly enjoyed and was greatly enjoyable speaking on non-political subjects: on William Booth, Shakespeare, his beloved Scott, the *Boys' Own Paper*, geologists or William Morris he seldom failed to produce an original nugget or two, or sometimes an intuition of a De la Mare quality. He spoke for instance of the familiar thrill of sniffing the misty air of the sea after being pent in a city or of finding oneself amid the eternal snows of the Alps – they, he said, strike 'some chord that goes back a thousand years, to the time when our ancestors lived in a country which was under snow half the year, or came from the Friesian coasts where the waves are always rolling . . .'

During the years when he was Lord President, his life fell into an agreeable pattern and he had time to indulge his liking for cricket, music and of course books. He popped quietly down to Cambridge from time to time to dine at one or other of the colleges and once with a club called 'The Family', where he sat next to A. E. Housman, poet and professor of Latin. Although Housman was a Worcestershire man Baldwin found him 'most unclubbable'. 'I could get nothing out of him, was told after I could have drawn him with obscene stories, but I gave them up when I left Harrow.' Perhaps the food was better than the conversation – and Baldwin, though neither gourmet nor gourmand, enjoyed food in the best English styles. He remembered a lunch he had given Laval at No. 10 in 1935: 'I didn't attempt to compete with French cooking. We had salmon trout, mixed grill, very mixed, Kentucky ham which tasted like crystallized nectar, plum pudding and brandy sauce.' He thought gaily that if Hitler ever came, he should give him haggis and whisky.

It was a nicely balanced mode of existence and it always included the consolations and comforts of prayer and belief in God. He still at sixty-eight thought intensely that God would make use of him, although, he told Jones, 'as one grew old, one's prayers became shorter – just sighs and interjections'. All in all he could look back on a life which, he told schoolboys of the Leys School in Cambridge, had been 'progressively happier, far more interesting as time has gone on, for all its cares and its anxieties'.

When he said that he had just emerged from a situation that might have ended his public life abruptly and ignominiously.

6

PRIME MINISTER DEFAMED

1935–1947

THE WHIRLWIND that came near to destroying Baldwin and his Government blew up at the end of 1935 over some proposals, made jointly by Sir Samuel Hoare, the British Foreign Secretary, and his French counterpart, Pierre Laval, to settle the Italian war against Abyssinia, which began on 3 October. Abyssinia, or Ethiopia, was an African slave-owning country – so barbarous that Britain had protested against her entry into the League – at the southern end of the Red Sea, bordering the Anglo-Egyptian Sudan, Kenya and British Somaliland, and dividing the two Italian provinces of Eritrea and Somaliland. The country was 'ruled' by an Emperor whose writ in reality scarcely ran outside his palace gates in Addis Ababa.

Italy invaded Abyssinia, not without plenty of warning, to seize some of her territories and to revenge her defeat many years before at Adowa, but also because Benito Mussolini, the Italian dictator and former Socialist agitator, needed to provide his people with a grand 'show' and the spoils of war. Baldwin at first mildly observed that 'in dealing with Signor Mussolini we are not dealing with a normal kind of intellect'. After Mussolini had used poison gas against the Abyssinians Baldwin was firmer: 'The man is a savage.' Later he simply categorized him as 'lunatic'.

Before Mussolini launched his invasion in October 1935, the British Cabinet, by agreement with the League of Nations, sent Eden, then No. 2 in the Foreign Office, to Rome to attempt to buy him off by offering him the Abyssinian lowlands, and offering Abyssinia in return part of British Somaliland, thus giving her the outlet to the Red Sea which she lacked. Mussolini refused because he wanted in particular the territory bordering Kenya and the Sudan which had minerals and lush plains.

Must it, then, be sanctions and war under the Covenant? Baldwin stood firmly in support of action by the League, despite a far from unanimous Cabinet and despite warnings from Warren Fisher, head of the Civil Service and the Treasury, that his 'belligerence' could lead to catastrophe: 'Is England really prepared not merely to threaten, but also to use force, and is she in a position to do this successfully?' he enquired. Chatfield, the First Sea Lord, said the British Fleet could defeat Italy but, since Italy's Air Force was equipped with torpedo bombers, might lose four capital ships: what then of the defence of the Empire and the Far East?

Nevertheless, in September 1935 Baldwin sent Hoare to Geneva to tell the League of Nations that Britain stood under the Covenant for 'steady and collective resistance to all acts of unprovoked aggression'. Hoare carefully put particular emphasis on *'collective'*, striking the desk of the rostrum as he did so. He and Baldwin knew that with Germany, Japan and the USA out of the League there could be no collective resistance; it would come down in the end to Britain and France doing the job, and both men knew that France would not act since she regarded Italy as her most important ally in the event of war with Germany, and Italy was already on bad terms with Germany because, during the abortive Nazi *putsch* against Austria, Mussolini had rushed troops to the frontier.

Still, forlorn hope as it was, Baldwin gave the League a lead by sending a large part of the British Home Fleet, including two battle cruisers, to Gibraltar. The lead was not followed by France nor by any other League member. The Dominions would not fight. Britain was alone: 'Not a ship, not a machine, not a man has been moved by any other member State,' said Hoare. Baldwin repeated, on the day Mussolini launched his invasion, that 'His Majesty's Government have not, and have never had, any intention of taking isolated action in this dispute . . . The responsibility for any action that may be taken rests on all and must be faced squarely by all.'

Baldwin saw the position with great clarity: 'We could cut Italy's communications, but if Mussolini broke out, there would be more killed in Valletta [Malta] in one night than in all the Abyssinian campaign up to date and until we got an agreement with the French we should have to go on fighting the Italians single-handed for a month or so. French mobilization would have led to riots. They are not ready in the air without mobilization,' he told Tom Jones. Nor, of course, was Britain ready; the three bases she would require – Malta, Alexandria and Base X, i.e. Navarino – were virtually defenceless, the fleet undermanned, A.A. ammunition scarce. Besides, Baldwin was concerned with building up Britain's forces, not having them broken down, particularly when this would so expose her weakness as to destroy her precarious credit as a world power. Vansittart in his autobiography went so far as to say that 'there is little doubt that we should have lost the Second World War, and ceased to be a nation, if we had spent our small naval margins prematurely'.

There were other considerations. Britain had no vital, or strategic, interest involved in Abyssinia nor in smashing Italy, an old ally. A Foreign Office committee, chaired by Sir John Maffey, considered the implications of the increase of Italian armaments passing into the Red Sea, and reported that an Italian conquest of Abyssinia would not affect Britain's Imperial interests, except possibly for the headwaters of the Nile, which watered Egypt, and were gathered in Abyssinian territory at Lake Tsana. On the other hand Britain had every interest in avoiding making an enemy on the main line of communications to the Far East and in not encouraging Mussolini to turn to Hitler for support: that would be the height of folly. Then again, though Baldwin had many times stated that collective support of the League of Nations was the lynch-pin of British foreign policy, the League's record – over the Italian assault on Corfu, and the Japanese invasion of Manchuria – was not such as to dispose knowledgeable observers, including Baldwin, to place much faith in it. The Covenant itself was hastily cobbled up, full of legal loopholes, and was in any case an experiment with no real precedent. The peace had been kept, where it was kept, by the *pax Romana* or the *pax Britannica*, all-powerful Empires, or by diplomatic manoeuvring among the interested parties. The League, on the other hand, could logically find itself in the position of, as the American H. E. Barnes put it, 'making perpetual war for perpetual peace'. Even its weapon of economic sanctions, that is blockade, could lead to war.

Such sanctions were now applied against Italy. They had little effect. But, it was argued, an embargo on her oil supplies would do the trick. Perhaps; on the other hand it might force Mussolini into doing a 'mad dog' act with an attack on the British Fleet which, after all, was the only real target readily available to him. This Baldwin hesitated to risk and so he turned to older methods of bringing about peace: that secret diplomacy, unjustly thought of as a cause of the 1914–18 war, which perhaps because it had grown rusty turned out to be not so very secret. Where possible, negotiation would be done under League auspices.

Baldwin never concealed the existence of this two-pronged policy, and Hoare stated it openly in the Commons on 5 December: he had 'consistently and steadily followed the double line that has time after time been approved by the League and this House. On the one hand we have taken our full part in the collective action under the Covenant, and on the other hand we have continued our efforts for a peaceful settlement.' Such a settlement meant compromise, an offer favourable enough to Mussolini to induce him to stop the war. A plan must be contrived between Britain and France, the two directly interested parties. But the minutes of the Cabinet meeting on 2 December only mentioned in passing that it was agreed to 'press on by every useful means with discussions with the countries concerned, with a view to a peaceful settlement'; most of the discussion centred on oil sanctions and the need to avoid war.

Now the drama began. Hoare told his colleagues that he was run down, and his doctor recommended a brief holiday, which he proposed to begin that coming Saturday, 7 December. Baldwin, as always, was sympathetic: 'Have a good leave and get your health back. That is the most important thing,' he said. Hoare was going to skate in Switzerland – he was a silver-medal skater – and he casually mentioned to Baldwin that as Laval, the French Prime Minister and Foreign Minister, had been pressing for a meeting, he would break his journey in Paris: 'By all means,' said Baldwin. 'Push Laval as far as you can, but on no account get this country into war.' The Cabinet minutes of 2 December refer specifically to Hoare's brief: 'If the peace talks did not offer any reasonable prospect of a settlement or if the military conversations showed that France was not willing to cooperate, he [Hoare] was to bring "the question" back for consideration by the Cabinet.' Hoare's colleagues hoped 'that he would take a generous view of the Italian attitude'.

Baldwin and the Cabinet discussed no details of a possible settlement, though they were constantly under consideration in the Foreign Office, one of whose officers, Maurice Peterson, had for some time been negotiating with his French opposite numbers; these negotiations focused on variations of the plan put to Mussolini by Eden some months earlier. It is clear that Vansittart, the Permanent Under-Secretary, was determined on a peaceful settlement with Italy to restore the Stresa Front, and that he and Hoare regarded the meeting with Laval much more seriously than did Baldwin. Hoare left a message behind for the Foreign Office saying bluntly: 'We intend to go all out for bringing the conflict to an end ...'; he hoped to agree with Laval 'a basis for a peace negotiation'.

Hoare stumbled off to Paris, there to be joined by Vansittart, the British Ambassador Sir George Clerk, and Peterson. He talked for two days with Laval and between them they concocted a plan – it could never be more than a plan since any proposal had to be accepted by the Cabinet, Abyssinia, Italy and the League. Abyssinia was to cede to Italy not only the territory she had already gained by arms but also regions further east – some 50,000 square miles – and give Italy 'exclusive economic rights' in a vast area to the south. Abyssinia in return was to receive with full sovereign rights an outlet to the sea, preferably by Italian cession of a strip of Eritrea or, as in the Eden plan, a corridor through British Somaliland to the sea. The Emperor would retain his old kingdom in the mountains.

A communiqué was issued, saying merely that 'formulae' had been sought. But when Eden, in charge at the Foreign Office, saw a transcript of the first day's talks, he was alarmed; the final transcript coincided with a leakage of the complete proposals in two French newspapers. When the British newspapers printed what had been leaked in France – and condemned it – there was a great hue and cry, an outburst of moral indignation, from as diverse quarters as the League of Nations Union, the two Archbishops, and *The Times*. Their naïve belief in the League as a defence against war had been rudely set aside, apparently to be replaced by *Realpolitik*. There was, then, after all no morality in the relationship between states, and so, they argued, war had been brought measurably nearer. Protesting letters and telegrams rained onto Baldwin's desk. He was seen to throw them into the air with the angry cry: 'Tell the press we must have more aeroplanes.' But he refused to see the press, even Geoffrey Dawson of *The Times*, and withdrew himself as though to listen to inner voices rather than the tumult outside. But the voices were unclear whereas the shouting was clear enough.

Even some Conservative MPs were shocked. The Chief Whip bluntly told Baldwin: 'Our men won't stand for it'; among those men was an outraged Austen Chamberlain. 'It was', Baldwin told the Cabinet, 'a worse situation in the House of Commons than he had ever known.' There he could only disconsolately murmur that he could not yet reveal anything until the matter had been before the League and the parties concerned. My lips, he said, are 'not yet unsealed', but when the troubles were past he could 'guarantee that not a member would go into the Lobby against us'. Later he admitted that it was 'one of the stupidest things I ever said' (though one of the things he could not disclose was real enough – the Secret Intelligence Service had reported to him that Laval had been taking money from Mussolini).

Worse was to come. In Cabinet, Cunliffe-Lister, Secretary for Air, threatened to resign over this 'staggering and demoralizing episode'. More than half his colleagues agreed with him, and Baldwin's friend Halifax, of whom he once said 'we talk the same language', went so far as to say that it was not merely Hoare's position that was in doubt: 'If the Prime Minister were to lose his personal position, one of our national anchors would have dragged.' Baldwin was in great danger: if Hoare was not given his marching orders, then the Cabinet would withdraw their support and the Prime Minister would have to resign. Baldwin afterwards told Tom Jones that he was 'knocked sideways. For two days I did not know where I stood'.

Hoare returned from Switzerland but was confined to bed; he had suffered a blackout while skating and had broken his nose. Neville Chamberlain went to tell him what the Cabinet had been saying and urged him to recant his views on the peace scheme. He would not: 'I was convinced', wrote Hoare in his autobiography, 'that nothing short of the proposals would save Abyssinia and prevent Musslini from joining the Hitler front.' That evening Hoare resigned; he had not exactly been sacked but the Cabinet view, as conveyed by Neville Chamberlain, left him little alternative. Meanwhile Baldwin saw Austen Chamberlain, the former

Foreign Secretary and veteran back-bencher who had become the spearhead of Conservative opposition to the Hoare–Laval plan, and said: 'When Sam has gone I shall want to talk to you about the Foreign Office.' The hint was broad enough; Chamberlain imagined he was to be recalled to office.

On Thursday, 19 December, Hoare made a magnificent and realistic defence of the plan, and would, some thought, have carried the House if he had still been Foreign Secretary. He put the position in a nutshell: 'It is a choice between the full cooperation of all member states [of the League] and the kind of unsatisfactory compromise that was contemplated in the suggestions which M. Laval and I put.' His plan, indeed, was perfectly sensible; and Baldwin might have done well to back him rather than, in effect, sack him. Now, as a result of one of Britain's periodical fits of morality, negotiation or secret diplomacy was discredited and at the same time collective military action was rejected by all militarily powerful members of the League. So Italy annexed the whole of Abyssinia on 9 May 1936, and Mussolini proclaimed a new Roman Empire. Vansittart summed it up pungently: under the Hoare–Laval proposals, 'the aggressor was getting more than he had, though less than he would take.' He now took the lot, to the admiration and encouragement of Hitler, and the League faltered into fatuity until, in September 1939, no one bothered to tell it officially that war had broken out.

Baldwin spoke after Hoare in the Commons. He was visibly shaken, and his speech, though frank, was one of his poorest: 'It was feeble, toneless and unhappy,' wrote G. M. Young. Baldwin said that the Hoare–Laval proposals went too far: 'I was not expecting that deeper feeling that was manifest in many parts of the country on what I may call the grounds of conscience and of honour ... It is perfectly obvious now that the proposals are absolutely and completely dead ... I had done something that was not wise or right.' The climb-down was ignominious and Baldwin 'wore the air of a man crushed by some appalling disaster'. Yet, he had listened to the voice of the people even if the people had in part been manoeuvred by newspapers and unscrupulous politicians.

The Parliamentary day was saved by none other than Austen Chamberlain, perhaps encouraged by Baldwin's broad hint. Chamberlain knew that he could have so reduced Baldwin's majority as to force his resignation, but he did not. Rather he picked on what Attlee had said about the 'honour' of the Prime Minister being questionable. For that reason, said Chamberlain, he would vote for the Government. The Government majority was 397 to 165.

Hoare's departure defused the political tension; it did not clear Baldwin's conscience from the guilty feeling that he had briefed Hoare insufficiently and then sacrificed him to save himself – a feeling not confined to Baldwin's conscience alone. Penitentially he determined to bring Hoare back into the Cabinet as soon as opportunity offered. Nor could Baldwin soon forgive himself for having, for once in his life, mistaken the mood of Parliament and people, with the result that his personal prestige dived. Perhaps he was losing his touch? At any rate he now, for him, behaved oddly. As promised before the debate on Hoare's resignation speech, he saw Austen Chamberlain, but to tell him that the Foreign Office was to go to Eden: 'If you had been ten years younger, there would have been no doubt in my mind...' Chamberlain could however, if he wished, become a Minister of State to advise on foreign policy and defence. 'He told me I was ga-ga,' spluttered Chamberlain when he retailed the story. 'Physically unfit for hard work and he feared I might become as much of an incubus as MacDonald.' All he wanted was 'the use of my name to patch up the damaged reputation of the Government'. Chamberlain, who at seventy-four was only four years older than Baldwin, waxed furious; he wrote to his sister Ida that Baldwin was 'self-centred, selfish and idle' and ' "Sly, Sir, devilish sly!" ' Even Baldwin's appointment of Eden was ungraceful. After asking Eden who was the best man to be Foreign Office Secretary and dismissing the names he suggested, Baldwin said: 'It looks as if it will have to be you.' It was quite out of his normal courteous style.

The crisis, of course, had brought some gains. The public, Baldwin thought, had learned that it was not enough for all countries to shout 'stop' to an aggressor and that League members had to be rearmed before 'collective security' would work. All the same, whatever excuses could be made, the affair had been disastrous. Now new tribulations were about to fall upon the shoulders of a man who, examined by the doctor Lord Dawson of Penn, was found to be physically in order but with 'an inclination to get tired sooner than usual'. On 20 January, King George V died only a few months after the astonishing expression of popular admiration for him at his Silver Jubilee celebrations, and before long his departure was to lead to another crisis. Baldwin spoke of him on the wireless as a 'wise and loving friend and counsellor' who played to the end a gallant part in 'the raving world'. It was a moving, homely tribute. Neville Chamberlain thought it went far to restore Baldwin's reputation. People listening would, he believed, have said: 'This is the man we trust; he may be slow, but he is honest and sincere and cares for the same things as we do.'

Yet his normal confidence and calm did not quickly come back, and the death of his cousin Kipling further depressed him. He was insufficiently firm, some thought, in pushing the Defence Requirements Committee's recommendations for increase in all arms of the Services, to cost £394m. over five years. Baldwin announced the expanded programme on 27 February 1936, and this was hailed as the beginning of real British rearmament. However, the debate on the White Paper in March 1936 showed that whatever the country had learned from the Italian aggression, the Labour Party chiefs had learned nothing. Their resolution began: 'The safety of this country and the peace of the world cannot be secured by reliance on armaments but only by the resolute pursuit of a policy of international understanding, adherence to the Covenant of the League of Nations, general disarmament, the progressive improvement of international labour standards, and economic cooperation so as to remove the causes of war.'

This sort of brick wall Baldwin had faced too often to allow it to deter him, however down in the dumps he might be, and he now decided that the time was ripe to create a Minister for the Coordination of Defence. Despite Austen Chamberlain's public pleading for Winston Churchill to fill the post, Baldwin appointed Sir Thomas Inskip, the Attorney General. The appointment was jeered at by the more militant Conservatives. Yet there would have been small support then for Churchill, who, always seeking the limelight, might have done more harm than good. In fact Inskip's clear mind cut through many an inter-Services tangle and a dozen financial knots; it was his memorandum to the Cabinet that ended the obsession with bombers and gave greater priority to fighters, without which the Battle of Britain would have been lost.

On 7 March 1936, Hitler, who had been off the world scene for a time, sent 30,000 troops into the Rhineland, which had been demilitarized and, for a time, occupied by Allied troops after Versailles, though it had remained under German civil administration. This was Hitler's riposte to the French ratification of the Franco–Soviet pact on 27 February 1936. Under the Locarno Treaty, Britain, France and Italy should have rushed to resist the re-occupiers, but they could not and did not. Moreover, Hitler had combined his re-militarization with fair-seeming offers of various non-aggression pacts, though all petered out later. In Britain there was almost no backing for military action or sanctions. 'Why shouldn't a man go into his own backyard?' people asked. Dalton, Labour's spokesman on foreign affairs, was quite open about it: 'It is only right to say bluntly and frankly that public opinion in this country would not support the taking of military sanctions or even economic sanctions against Germany at this time, in order to put German troops out of the Rhineland.' What a change was there! Dalton's speech was conveniently forgotten by those Socialists who subsequently used the Rhineland as an early example of appeasement. Baldwin was truly representing British opinion when he told the Cabinet that military action was inappropriate, 'out of proportion to what Germany had done'.

Hotfoot from Paris steamed Flandin, who had succeeded Laval as Foreign Minister, for a private meeting with Baldwin. Flandin, though in a minority in his own Cabinet, wanted all out sanctions; he was sure there would be no risk of war. Baldwin replied: 'You may be right, but if there is one chance in a hundred that war will result from your police operation I have not the right to involve England because' – there he hesitated, and Flandin noticed what it cost him to make the admission – 'Britain is not in a state to go to war.' (It is known now that Flandin was right in believing that Germany would not fight and would withdraw. It was not known then.) Baldwin gave Flandin facts and figures, among them the British Joint Planners' estimate that Britain could only put two divisions into the field, and these without tanks, anti-tank guns or mortars. Combined French and British air strength available was put at 306 bombers and 469 fighters. So, with the reoccupation of the Rhineland, Versailles and Locarno crumbled like pressed flowers in an old book; the Stresa Front had already broken up with Italy's invasion of Abyssinia. Britain, however, still held herself bound to give France assistance were she directly attacked.

But surely, surely war need not happen? 'Hitler, the dictator of Germany, has it in his power today', said Baldwin in a speech in April 1936, 'to do more at this moment to lift the black shadow of fear from Europe than any other man living . . . God grant that he may have the will.' Once more Baldwin thought he might talk with Hitler himself. He wanted better relations with him, as he told Eden, and he sympathized with his fear of encirclement. His friend Tom Jones had seen Hitler, who had talked soberly and wanted to meet Baldwin, and Ribbentrop repeated the invitation; perhaps they could meet on a ship near Dover or in some 'mountainous rendezvous'. Baldwin was much taken by the thought of meeting the strange, evil little genius because personal knowledge alone, he believed, would enable him to see clearly how to act. But he insisted on Eden, the Foreign Secretary, accompanying him, and Eden warned him that Hitler's real object was to divide Britain from France. The idea faded away and no meeting took place.

A different sort of thought began to germinate in his mind. In Russia, the dictator Stalin was carrying out a nation-wide purge – by execution or imprisonment – of the old Bolshevik leaders and Army chiefs; the numbers ran into hundreds of thousands. To Baldwin the Russian terror seemed as evil as that of the Nazis, but fortunately the Nazis gave every appearance of wishing to destroy the Russians. That being so, he told one young Conservative, Vice-Admiral Hughes-Hallett, 'he could not believe that British diplomacy would be so inept as to become involved in war with either of them, until they were at each other's throats. Then we could see how it went for a while'. Such thoughts could not be passed on to a public of whom a considerable minority, stirred up by the left Book Club and fellow-travelling MPs, still saw Russia as the promised land. Baldwin did not wish to alienate any section of the public; he sought to lead them to a bipartisan attitude to foreign affairs.

But Baldwin spoke more openly to a meeting in July 1936 of eighteen Conservatives, members of the Commons, the Lords and the Privy Council, and led by Churchill. He had hoped for Labour and Liberal members also, but their leaders declined. Still, it was a delegation of weight and intelligence. To pointed questions on rearmament, Baldwin replied that none of their anxieties had not weighed with him, 'day and night for the last four years'. One difficulty was to get the public to understand such anxieties; a greater difficulty was to judge what was going on in the mind of that 'strange man' Hitler. No one really knew. According to *Mein Kampf*, he planned to move east, and if he did 'I shall not break my heart'. Baldwin added: 'I do not believe he wants to move west, because west would be a very difficult programme for him.'

But supposing Hitler went mad; could diplomacy work against that? There was dubious value in his pledges. So if Germany attacked Russia and France went to Russia's aid, as she was bound by treaty to do, what should Britain do? That question Churchill answered for him: if Britain detached herself from France she could pair up with Germany. Baldwin did not disagree: 'I am not going to get this country into a war with anybody for the League of Nations or anybody else or for anything else. If there is any fighting to be done in Europe, I should like to see the Bolsheviks and the Nazis doing it.' Churchill did not demur.

Baldwin was tiring, too many people wanting his attention; too many secretaries seeking decisions, too many wearisome colleagues. Of course there were achievements to chalk up in the first half of 1936: the school-leaving age had been raised to fifteen, unemployment insurance extended to farm labourers, and slum clearance begun under the 1935 Act. Baldwin's enquiries two years before into the 'shirts' had resulted in the Public Order Act, which stopped the clashes between Mosley's blackshirts and the Communists. Yet to the compassionate eye of Baldwin many things were still wrong. In a few towns 80 per cent were unemployed; in West Auckland only one man in ten had worked in the previous seven years. Baldwin could still make winning speeches; his energy failed when it came to pushing remedial action and even Chamberlain thought the Reconstruction Bill was 'pretty thin'. He would give no lead in publicizing plans for the areas of great unemployment and young Conservative MPs started to criticize him publicly. He was silly enough to take notice of a minor cabal against him, much exaggerated by the newspapers, and refer to it as 'a time of year when midges come out of dirty ditches'. Even his old *fidus Achates*, Davidson, was constrained to tell him that 'among your most devoted supporters, is a vague feeling that there is some truth in the accusation of "lack of Cabinet control by the PM"'. Every mongrel is yapping, believing a very tired fox has gone to ground at Chequers with no fight left in him'.

Baldwin was, indeed, nearing breakdown once more. Tom Jones noticed 'his strained nervous condition showing itself in the game [Patience], banging the tiny cards on the table, venting on them the pent-up wrath which should have been poured on his colleagues ...' Baldwin was taking French phosphorus pills for nervous exhaustion, and he told Jones that he intended to retire after the Coronation on 12 May 1937. On the eve of his holiday came news of civil war in Spain between forces of the dubiously elected left-wing Popular Front Government and the Army, led by General Franco. Britain's policy, Baldwin agreed, would be non-intervention, and Eden embargoed the export of arms and aircraft to Spain. Germany and Italy, however, did intervene on the side of the Army and Russia began to help the left-wing forces. Volunteers went from Britain to join the left and the right. Baldwin disliked that; there were, he said, 'on either side, large bodies of men prepared to fight and die for an abstract creed. That is by far the most dangerous thing in the world today'. Before he left London he gave Eden the instruction 'that on no account, French or other, must he bring us in to fight on the side of the Russians', to whom the French under its left-wing Government led by Léon Blum inclined.

Baldwin decided against Aix for his holiday, and early in August 1936 begain a long round of country house visits in England and Wales – Blickling, Lord Lothian's country house in Norfolk, at Cark with the Cavendishes, at Longleat. Walking with a friend one day in Westmorland and talking about the beauties around them, he suddenly stopped in his tracks and said: 'I cannot think what is happening to me, I seem to be losing the use of my legs. It's the unbearable responsibility that gets me down', and, wrote his friend: 'He was tense and withdrawn. He stood and gazed at the hills and I began to feel like an intruder.' Gradually the silence of the hills brought its customary healing and Baldwin, much restored, returned to Downing Street on 12 October 1936.

On his desk was a pile of letters and cuttings from American newspapers about the new King's association with an American divorcee, Mrs Bessie Wallis Simpson, née Warfield, aged forty. Photographs in the newspapers showed them bathing together on beaches in Dalmatia and sailing together aboard a luxury yacht, the *Nahlin*. *Time* magazine dubbed her 'Queen Wally' and said that the King would marry her when she was free from her present husband, Ernest Simpson. So far the British press had kept silent, but no one knew for how long.

Did it, Baldwin asked himself, mean anything or was it a passing infatuation? The King at forty-one had emerged safely from close friendships with several married women, Lady Coke, Mrs Freda Dudley Ward, Thelma Furness. He had shown no inclination to marry; in the eyes of the adoring public he was still the wistful, golden-haired Prince Charming waiting for the Fairy Queen. Baldwin had liked him from the time of their trip together to Canada in 1927, and Davidson observed that 'they could well be regarded as friends', in so far as their separation in years would allow.

Yet Baldwin had reservations about the Prince. Although he had worked without stint in Britain and the Empire, he had gloomy fits when he cut appointments, or was unpunctual, and as early as 1927 Baldwin had been asked by a high official of the Prince's household to use his influence to correct these faults, and perhaps such others as the wearing of unorthodox clothes – he had to the end of his life a penchant for bright colours and large patterns – and his devotion to the 1920s nightclubbing craze. A strange incident occurred when King George v was close to death in February 1928, and the Prince had to be recalled from East Africa. Baldwin met him at Folkestone and on the journey to London the Prince said he hoped that Baldwin would always speak freely to him on any subject whatsoever. Baldwin replied: 'Sir, I shall remind you of that,' and a curious presentiment came over him 'that one day he most certainly should have something to say to him, and that it would be about a woman'.

Another flash of his Celtic second-sight came to him when he first heard London society gossip about the Prince and Mrs Simpson. He remarked to a friend: 'When I was a little boy in Worcestershire reading history books I never thought I should have to interfere between a King and his mistress.' Baldwin had ever since suffered twinges of anxiety about the Prince; these were not assuaged when shortly before his death King George told Baldwin of his fear that 'after I am dead the boy will ruin himself within twelve months'. On the day of Edward's accession Baldwin mentioned to Attlee his doubts whether the new King 'would stay the course'. To Tom Jones in the same month he observed that he, Baldwin, being a 'scrimshanker', had hoped to escape the responsibility of taking charge of the Prince as King but, he added, 'perhaps Providence has kept me here for that purpose'.

Mrs Simpson was not the only problem. As soon as the Prince became King he, quite naturally, sought to alter some of the rigid routines of his father and to cut away some of the protocol, but he was impatient and tactless about it. He reduced the royal staff, summarily dismissing old and loyal retainers, and cut the pay of those remaining. Lord Wigram, the King's Private Secretary, resigned because, he told Baldwin, he found the King's 'temper and habits so irregular'; he was succeeded by his assistant, Alex Hardinge, and he in the end no longer enjoyed his master's confidence. Though in earlier days as Prince, Edward had been generous, now he became stingy, except when buying presents of jewellery or furniture for Mrs Simpson, which he did almost daily; to meet her he would drop public engagements. He took only a desultory interest in the official boxes of papers yet sought to interfere with Cabinet decisions, notably over the German remilitarization of the Rhineland – a fact Eden admitted to Jan Masaryk, the Czech ambassador, in October 1936. The King was against any military action to stop the Germans, as doubtless his father would have been, and as it happened the Cabinet was too; the point was that he had expressed it to the Cabinet as his wish instead of giving his opinion privately to the Prime Minister. The King was on terms of personal friendship with the German Ambassador in London, Leopold van Hoesch (who was not a Nazi).

Worse still, reports reached Baldwin from General Stuart Menzies, head of the Secret Intelligence Service (M.I.6.), that leakages of the contents of State Papers had been traced to the King; the matter came before the Cabinet but there is no mention of it in the minutes as made available. This did not necessarily implicate the King himself: the boxes, sent to his home at Fort Belvedere, near Sunningdale, were sometimes left unexamined for weeks by the monarch, but available to any domestic or other snooper. Mrs Simpson, too, came under suspicion of too close contact with the German Embassy and the security services were given a watching brief over her and her friends. Since she was constantly with the King, he too was under surveillance, an unprecedented situation. Soon despatch boxes sent to the King were being carefully screened by the Foreign Office and any highly secret matter excluded. Of course, many perfectly reputable people at that time preferred the Germans, even under Hitler, to the French, who were allied to the Russians, and it was quite *comme il faut* to say so and to seek to improve relations between the two countries – as indeed Baldwin himself had instructed Eden to do. But the King was in a different position.

Baldwin took no precipitate action. He even suppressed a draft memorandum (now lost) that Neville Chamberlain prepared to be sent to the King some time before the Simpson affair became pressing. It urged him to settle down, to wear conventional clothes, to work at his 'boxes' and not to make remarks in public about slums and unemployment. Chamberlain's paper, Baldwin thought, would have sent the King 'sky high and, I am sure, would have been a mistake'. All the same Chamberlain believed that unless the King 'pulled up his socks he will soon pull down the throne'. Baldwin as usual preferred to wait, since problems often solved themselves. Perhaps the King *would* settle down; perhaps his *grande passion* would die a natural death.

But this time Baldwin had mistaken his man. The King, though possessed of great charm and a capacity for hard work, had little intelligence and less common sense. Like many of his family he was stubborn and perhaps, in his heart of hearts, he did not want to be King, though he later denied this. His duties were onerous and perhaps he could not bear the thought of having to carry them out for the next thirty or forty years until he died. Baldwin gave a character sketch of him to his niece, Monica Baldwin, a year after the abdication:

He is an abnormal being, half-child, half-genius. It is almost as though two or three cells in his brain had remained entirely undeveloped while the rest of him is a mature man. He is not a *thinker*. He takes his ideas from the daily press instead of thinking things out for himself. He never reads – except, of course, the papers. No serious reading: none at all. He is *reasonable*: that is to say, when he really *sees* a thing, he does it. You might say he is amenable to reason – except, of course, on that one subject . . .

Baldwin added: 'He has no religious sense. I have never in my life met anyone so completely lacking in any sense of the – the – well, what is *beyond*'.

Events in October began to take what afterwards seemed a predestined course. On the 15th Mrs Simpson filed a petition for divorce on the grounds of her husband's misconduct at a hotel in Bray with a woman called Buttercup Kennedy. The petition was due to be heard on 27 October at Ipswich Assizes because the London court lists were full for a year ahead. After that and the legal six months' interval, Mrs Simpson would be free to marry again. Did the King really intend to marry her? Still Baldwin shrank from broaching the subject. At last, pushed by the advice of 'two old friends and wise men', Lord Salisbury and Edmund Talbot, he arranged a meeting with the King for the morning of 20 October.

'I motored over from Chequers,' he told Tom Jones. 'It was a most beautiful morning, and St Luke's Day, and I felt like a physician. I was received in his study. I had warned Hardinge to prepare the King for the subject of my visit. I began by telling him that on his accession he had been good enough to say that he was glad I was Prime Minister and his counsellor. Did he still think so? And was he willing to listen to counsel where a woman was concerned? The King responded: he was. So I went ahead.' After talking of the large correspondence he had on the King's relations with Mrs Simpson, he said:

'I think I know our people. They'll tolerate a lot in private life, but they will not stand for this sort of thing in the life of a public personage, and when they read in the *Court Circular* of Mrs Simpson's visit to Balmoral they resented it.' The King: 'The lady is my friend and I do not wish to let her in by the back door, but quite openly. I hope you will agree that I have carried out my duties as King with dignity.' The P.M.: 'I do agree and all the more as I know that the duties of royalty are not much to your liking. Cannot you have this coming divorce put off?' The King: 'That is the lady's private business.' I then went on to urge that Mrs Simpson should be asked to leave the country for six months, hoping that in the meantime the King's passion might cool and that other influences might be brought to play upon him. At some stage I suddenly interrupted the talk by asking: 'Do you think I could have a whisky and soda,' and adding: 'I do not find this conversation exactly an easy one to carry on.' The King himself refused to take any drink.

Baldwin pointed out that the British press would eventually break its silence. There might be sides taken, factions 'where no factions ought ever to exist'. Strangely enough, the King's intentions towards Mrs Simpson were not mentioned by either man, though the King gave a lead, which Baldwin did not follow, when he said that Wallis Simpson was 'the only woman in the world for him and he could not live without her'. On 27 October Mrs Simpson was granted a *decree nisi* at Ipswich and the next morning, in one American paper, appeared the elegant headline, 'King's Moll Reno'd in Wolsey's Home Town'. The British press reported the divorce briefly among other divorces. Baldwin's reaction, referring to Wolsey, was that 'he could quite understand why people were put in the Tower in the old days, and he would gladly put Mrs S. there if he could'.

Once more Baldwin waited on events, much to the dismay of his colleagues, who feared that the press could not long be restrained. Meantime he sought opinions and found them almost overwhelmingly against the King. He let the King's Private Secretary hint to his master that the Government might resign over the affair and the Opposition would refuse to form a Government. This could result only in a General Election which would inevitably be fought over the King's actions; there would be an extensive display of dirty washing. At this point Australia and Canada declared unequivocally that if there was any question of the King marrying Mrs Simpson and retaining his throne, they would not recognize it or him.

On 16 November, Baldwin summoned up courage to see the King again and this time was told bluntly: 'I mean to abdicate and marry Mrs Simpson.' So now the matter was in the open between them. Baldwin expressed his shock and grief for the Empire, but made no impression. The King was 'in an exalted frame of mind which nothing could ever shake'. Baldwin, according to his niece, even went so far as to ask: 'Was it absolutely necessary that he should *marry* her? In their peculiar circumstances, certain things are sometimes permitted to royalty which are not allowed to the ordinary man. To this he replied immediately: "Oh, there's no question of that. I am going to marry her . . ." The King was in a curious state of mind. He kept on repeating over and over again: "I can't do my job without her. I am going to marry her, and I will . . ." '

As yet there was no note of absolute finality and the King went off on a long-arranged two-day visit of the South Wales mining areas. There he expressed his sympathy with the unemployed: 'Something must be done to meet the situation in South Wales,' he told one miner, 'and I will do all I can to assist you.' The miners cheered him warmly. This was unfortunate because it made the King think that his popularity was such that he could ride over Baldwin, marry Mrs Simpson and keep his throne. Next day the *Daily Mail* contrasted 'His Majesty's solicitude for the unemployed in South Wales with the indifference of his Ministers', and an embryonic King's party began to build up.

The pace quickened. The King asked Baldwin, what about a morganatic marriage? Baldwin replied that he believed Parliament would never pass the Bill required. The King insisted and Baldwin warned him that he would have to put the matter to the whole Cabinet and the Dominions; once they had given their advice the matter would pass from the informal to the formal – and the King would be bound constitutionally by the formal advice forthcoming. Whether the King understood this or not, he asked Baldwin to do it and Baldwin acquiesced. The Cabinet (Duff Cooper only dissenting) and the Dominions rejected the proposal.

During the evening of 1 December, the Crystal Palace, that shining memorial of Victorian stability, burned to the ground, leaving only its twin towers standing, and on the morning of 2 December British press silence on the King's affair was at last broken. The same evening Baldwin again saw the King to tell him of the Cabinet's rejection of the morganatic scheme. So the either-or choice was in the open: renounce Mrs Simpson or abdicate. Small wonder that at this meeting Baldwin found the King fractious and irresponsible: 'To all arguments based on responsibility towards his people', Mrs Baldwin's diary records, 'the King did not react, not feeling any responsibility which should dictate or influence his conduct.' Or, as Baldwin explained to his niece: 'I appealed to one thing after another. Nothing made the least impression. It was almost uncanny: like talking to a child of ten years old. He did not seem to grasp the issues at stake. He seemed *bewitched* ... And he kept on repeating over and over again: "I can't do my job without her – I am going to marry her, and I will *go*." There was simply no moral struggle. It appalled me.'

Next day, 3 December, at Question Time Baldwin parried inquiries on the 'King's Matter' (as the Archbishop of Canterbury termed it), saying it was inexpedient at that time for him to be questioned. In the evening he again visited the King. Now the

King had another ploy: neither he nor Mrs Simpson insisted that she should be Queen, but he wanted to broadcast his desire to marry her and to suggest a brief withdrawal while the people reflected on the course they considered best. Baldwin was taken aback. The broadcast would be a straight appeal to the people over the heads of their elected representatives and how, in any case, were the people to make their views known? He had no doubt, he told the King, that the Cabinet would not agree to such a broadcast.

At last the naked cold steel wielded by Government struck the tin sword of the King and it fell out of his hand. The King said: 'You want me to go, don't you? And before I go, I think it is right, for her sake and mine, that I should speak.' Baldwin, seeking to soften the blow, replied with calm sympathy: 'What I want, Sir, is what you told me you wanted: to go with dignity, not dividing the country, and making things as smooth as possible for your successor. To broadcast would be to go over the heads of your Ministers and speak to the people. You will be telling millions throughout the world – among them a vast number of women – that you are determined to marry one who has a husband living. They will want to know all about her, and the press will ring with gossip, the very thing you want to avoid. You may, by speaking, divide opinion; but you will certainly harden it.' Even now Baldwin tried to avoid the dénouement. 'There is still time for you to change your mind, Sir. That indeed is the prayer of Your Majesty's servants.'

Baldwin felt compassion for the King in his appalling dilemma. Mrs Simpson had withdrawn to Cannes and the King, alone, almost isolated, was under great strain. Baldwin set out yet again on Tuesday evening, 7 December, for Fort Belvedere, prepared to wrestle with the King's conscience, if necessary all night in the old Methodist style. The King surprised him; he 'appeared happy and gay', Baldwin told the Cabinet, 'as if he were looking forward to his honeymoon'. The King was happy because his mind was finally made up. He was going. Now he could be magnanimous towards Baldwin: 'I quite understand the reason you and Mrs Baldwin don't approve of my action,' he told Baldwin as he was leaving the Fort. 'It is the view of another generation. My generation don't feel like that about it.' Baldwin could only express grief at the King's decision but he added that he and his wife hoped 'sincerely that you may find happiness where you believe it is to be found'.

Afterwards the ex-King was to say: 'The Prime Minister is the only man who has said any kind word to me about the future and wished me luck.'

The King signed the Instrument of Abdication on 10 December and at the dead of night left the country as Prince Edward, later to be the Duke of Windsor. So ended what H. L. Mencken called 'the greatest news story since the Resurrection'. With the crisis over Baldwin signalled its end in a masterly and conciliatory speech in the House of Commons. Before it he was nervous but recovered himself during the brief drive to the Commons; for, as he told Dugdale, his P.P.S.: 'This is making history and I am the only one who can do it.' It is surprising the speech ever got made at all. He had prepared some notes on scraps of paper; some of them were retrieved by his P.P.S. from the stairs at No. 10. The House was jammed with members whom he had to squeeze past to take his place on the Treasury bench. With him he had a red despatch box. After rummaging in his pocket he found the key, took out several sheets with the royal monogram, along with his own notes, and put them on the box in front of him. Hoare, now back in Government as First Lord, arrived at the box to answer Admiralty questions, and put his own papers on top of Baldwin's, which, when Hoare retired with his papers, fluttered to the floor, Baldwin bending down rather stiffly to pick them up.

He was heard in intense silence – the silence of Gettysburg, Harold Nicolson called it. The whole tenor of the speech, which was almost extempore, was to protect and preserve the crown which Edward's brother, George, now assumed. Baldwin defended the ex-King on the grounds that in all the circumstances he had behaved well (his occasional fractiousness was not mentioned). But just before the end of the speech Baldwin permitted himself these two sentences: 'I am convinced that where I have failed no one else could have succeeded. His mind was made up and those who know His Majesty know what that means.'

Nicolson, meeting him in a Commons corridor shortly after, diffidently praised him for his 'superb' performance. 'Yes, it was a success,' Baldwin agreed, 'I know it. It was almost wholly unprepared. I had a success, my dear Nicolson, at the moment I most needed it. Now is the time to go.' Not quite the time. That would come after the coronation of George on 2 May 1937. Meanwhile, in Mrs Baldwin's words, 'what we have all got to do is to set to work to repolish the throne!' It was done; within months rather than years, the shy and reluctant King George VI and his Queen Elizabeth sat on their thrones as if they had always been there.

Throughout the tense weeks Baldwin had scarcely put a foot wrong. Jones noted that 'he was in a much more decisive mood about this than about other political questions'. Perhaps he was secretly glad to be away from the ever-increasing turmoil of foreign affairs. He had very largely conducted matters alone, informing only three of four of his Cabinet colleagues, and this was to be held against him when the inevitable criticism came. Meanwhile he was buoyed up by evidence of general approval of his actions. But in the middle of the crisis, Lord Dawson of Penn told him: 'You will pay for this.' Payment, however, was deferred until his nervous collapse in the summer of 1937.

Baldwin, absorbed though he had been by the 'King's Matter,' had never ceased to be, actively, the Prime Minister. He was in on every policy decision on rearmament, leading the Cabinet, sorting out the confusion in Cabinet committees, talking to whoever had ideas. No detail escaped him; for instance, he saw that the Services Joint Planning Committee needed reinforcement if they were to do their job, and reinforced them. During 1936 rearmament progressed, though the Army remained the Cinderella of the Services, partly through Chamberlain's tight reign on expenditure, partly because Baldwin's appointment of his one-time saviour, Duff Cooper, as War Secretary had been less than successful. Cooper seemed incapable of asserting his will over his sleepy department and he made ill-judged use of the money available – for example, £44,000 was given to provide forage for horses, £12,000 for motor fuel. Baldwin shook his head over Cooper but did not replace him.

Baldwin replied on 14 November 1936 to an attack by Churchill alleging slowness in building up the Air Force; Churchill quoted figures of the German Air Force increases; the figures are now known to be exaggerated and were supplied by General Milch, Chief of the German Air Staff. Britain was ahead of, not behind Germany. During this speech Baldwin made his 'appalling frankness' statement; he could not have won an election on rearmament in 1933–4, he said. This was later twisted to suggest that he was referring to 1935, and was used against him in Churchill's history of the Second World War and elsewhere. Yet the words are clear enough, now as then. Rearmament remained Baldwin's particular care to the end of his premiership.

Foreign policy, unhappily, did not. The Cabinet agreed in July 1936 that Britain would defend Western Europe and the Empire, and that it was impossible to defend Eastern Europe as well. The object must be to get France and Italy to come to terms with Germany; Japan, the great threat in the Far East, must be deterred or brought into alliance. The failure was evident when Mussolini trumpeted the Rome–Berlin Axis on 1 November; and the anti-Comintern pact between Germany and Japan (later joined by Italy) was announced on 21 November. The positions that would prevail in the war were already being taken up. 'It is', wrote Hankey on 22 December, 'an appalling reflection on our foreign policy that we have lost our old friends, Japan and Italy, cannot get on terms with Germany and have as our only friend a France half-rotted with discontent and Communism.'

Some of the fault was that of Eden, the Foreign Secretary, still hankering after the dead League, but Baldwin cannot escape blame; he was Prime Minister and chairman of the Cabinet Foreign Policy Committee. He had left too much to Eden. When, for instance, Baldwin told him that 'we must get nearer to Germany', Eden asked: 'How?' Baldwin replied: 'I have no idea. That's your job.' Baldwin's intuitive feeling for home politics often deserted him when it came to divining the minds of foreigners. He had never forgotten Poincaré lying to him, nor the bad faith of Americans who, he noticed, were still refusing to cooperate with Britain over Japan. Mussolini and Hitler began by puzzling and intriguing him; in the end he dismissed them as two madmen, an insufficient judgement. Baldwin lacked the skills that, weighing this against that, produce a foreign policy.

His efforts in preparing the country for war cannot, however, be faulted. True, he resisted putting industry on a war footing and the setting up of a Ministry of Supply because they could not be done without some direction of labour, which would have alienated the unions as well as injuring trade and crippling the revenue on which, in the last resort, Britain would depend for financing a war if it came. But, almost his last decisive act, Baldwin presented a Defence White Paper in February 1937, which proposed an expenditure of some £1,500m., for which for the first time money was to be borrowed – some £400m. over five years. Deterrence, he explained, was the object, and 'ineffective deterrence is worse than useless'. The arms would never be used for aggression. They were to defend Britain, the Commonwealth, France and Belgium against unprovoked aggression. 'They may, and if a new Western Europe settlement can be reached, they would be used in defence of Germany were she the victim of unprovoked aggression by any other of the signatories of such a settlement.' These augmented forces would help any victim of aggression 'where in our judgement it would be proper under the provisions of the Covenant to do so'.

If, he said, war broke out it would 'run through Europe – the most terrible thing you can conceive – and if the forces are fairly even, you may have a repetition of 1914, with all its horror'. In short, parity is not enough; superiority is needed to win. Though Attlee, leader of the Opposition, said that 'I do not believe the Government are going to get any safety through these armaments ... We are obviously back to the law of the jungle', Baldwin's speech had its effect, for, during the next year, the Labour Party were belatedly to be converted from their habit of actually voting against the Service estimates instead of merely abstaining.

But a new leader was coming. Chamberlain would abandon the overwhelming superiority which the policy of deterrence demanded and retreat into the posture of defence, and this would mightily erode Britain's bargaining power. The drive behind rearmament would slacken – the Army estimates were actually reduced next year – and what Baldwin stood for would be undermined. He had one last go at the Imperial conference in May, painting a pessimsitic account of the dangers in Europe, but the delegates did not want to know; they worried much more about Japan and were fearful of a war on two fronts. To most of them, appeasement seemed the answer in Europe; they did not want to be involved.

Baldwin, limp and mentally tired out, was now counting the hours until release like a schoolboy, thought Jones, waiting for the holidays: 'Here I've been for fifteen years going to the House to answer fatuous questions.' He began to withdraw, but not with an air of 'calm of mind, all passion spent'. In his last public speech – it was at the Empire Rally of Youth at the Albert Hall – his phrasing was as felicitous as ever: 'I have had my hour. I pass soon into the shade . . .' – but what he had to say was far from bromide. Speaking to these young people from all over the world, he observed that 'it may well be that you have to save democracy from itself', and bluntly he told them that the League of Nations and the Versailles Treaty 'have belied the hope of mankind and given place to disillusion'; for good measure he pointed out that 'no State that ever was is worthy of a free man's worship'.

His last intervention in the Commons was on 5 May when with all his old conciliatory power he calmed down an ugly dispute at Hanworth Colliery which carried with it the threat of a national coal strike. He appealed to 'that handful of men, with whom rests war or peace, to rend and dissipate this dark cloud which has gathered over us, to show the world that this democracy at least can still practise the arts of peace in a world of strife'. The old magic, based on the trust the Opposition felt in Baldwin's fairness, worked again and a satisfactory settlement was made.

At the very last he introduced a bill to increase Ministers' salaries and – his own particular 'child' from 1925 – to give a salary to Leaders of the Opposition. The final Cabinet over which he presided agreed that MP's pay should be put up from £400 to £600 p.a., a 50 per cent rise. When he announced it in the Commons he was, naturally, cheered. 'So', wrote Harold Nicolson, 'his final words are to give us all £200 a year more. This means a lot to the Labour members and was done with Baldwin's usual consummate good taste. No man has ever left in such a blaze of affection.'

Baldwin resigned next morning, 28 May 1937, fourteen years to the day since he had been elected leader of his party. Next month he was created Earl Baldwin of Bewdley and Viscount Corvedale. 'There is', he remarked, 'perhaps a certain retributive justice in it as I have sent so many others there [to the Lords], hoping I should never see their faces again.' Presents were heaped upon him, including some fine wrought-iron gates for the main entrance to Astley Hall, but the one he most appreciated was the book Arthur Bryant wrote about him: 'I think', he told the historian, 'it made me happier than any letter I ever received.' Yet his premonitory faculties had not forsaken him; in reply to Halifax's congratulatory letter, he wrote: 'All hearts seem open for the moment: most will close again, some perhaps be kept ajar . . .' Baldwin, that lover of Rossetti's poetry, added: 'I still have that sense of wonder that the Blessed Damozel showed in her face as she leaned over the Golden Bar of Heaven. It wore off; so will mine. But it leaves something good, I hope, behind.'

The months that followed his departure and introduction to the House of Lords were full of the social round, speeches, dinners, though interrupted by his nervous collapse and his annual holiday in Aix, where he found he could no longer walk as once he did. Before the war he twice crossed the Atlantic to lecture. As for politics, he had said when relinquishing the premiership: 'Once I leave, I leave. I am not going to speak to the man on the bridge, and I am not going to spit on the deck.' In fact he did both, if by 'spitting' he meant criticizing policies. He spoke in the Lords after the Munich settlement in 1938, saying that he himself could not have gone to Munich but praising Chamberlain for having done so, and adding that no Prime Minister could commit his country to war until he was sure it was ready to fight.

Munich caused the resignation of Duff Cooper, by then First Lord of the Admiralty, who shortly wrote to his old sponsor begging him to return to the leadership because 'if the international situation deteriorates, which I believe it will, we shall be compelled to have a Coalition Government', and Baldwin was the only possible leader. Much the same sort of talk had taken place after Eden, the Foreign Secretary, resigned from the Government in February 1938, ostensibly over a minor matter, but really because he was discontented about Chamberlain's running his department for him.

Baldwin knew that he could not return; he was neither physically nor mentally able. He sensed, however, that something was wrong, that the country was not getting the lead it should from Chamberlain, who for all his powerful gifts was too shy, too curt and above all lacked Baldwin's vision. Others thought Baldwin could have done what Chamberlain could not. Davidson was later to comment: 'By 1937–8 Baldwin would have got Labour first to agree to some measure of direction of labour into defence interests, and I think when the situation had got as far as Munich he would have formed an absolutely united people facing Germany, and it is possible that there might well not have been war; I very much doubt that Hitler would have faced a showdown with a united Britain.' Baldwin still clung to a hope that Hitler could be turned east – 'Napoleon broke himself against the Russians. Hitler might do the same' (as eventually Hitler did). Meantime he worked hard for the fund which bore his name on behalf of the Jewish refugees from the Nazis, and raised no less than half a million pounds, for which the Nazis reviled him.

In August 1939, he crossed the Atlantic to lecture in New York. Returning, Baldwin and his wife intended to go to Aix but instead they went to Astley. German panzer troops had invaded Poland. The long-dreaded war came. In the first months Baldwin was active enough and kept well informed of the political scene; he shared the doubts of those who felt Chamberlain's conduct of hostilities inert and inept, and supported his replacement by Churchill whom, as we saw, he had 'kept on ice' for such an eventuality. Then came Dunkirk, and after that the bombers indeed got through to the ports and cities of Britain. The British were up against it; they responded bravely but also vilely. Led largely by such Socialists as A. L. Rowse, by left-wing papers like the *Daily Mirror* and by Michael Foot and Frank Owen in *Guilty Men*, they turned on Baldwin – Chamberlain being near to death – and accused him of not preparing the country for war, of betraying his trust, of being a traitor, practically of conspiring with Britain's enemies. He was picked as a scapegoat by the very people who had hissed and obstructed his rearmament programme, who had called him warmonger; by men who, as Harold Macmillan writes in *The Past Masters* (1975), were far more guilty than Baldwin.

As a result of this despicable campaign, he received letters of bitter abuse, which, since he no longer had a secretary, he opened himself. He did not complain even when local tradesmen seemed disinclined to serve the Baldwins. But when some gates and railings around his estate were requisitioned he did apply for their retention on grounds of artistic merit; this was turned down by the Minister of Public Buildings and Works, Lord Reith (not, as has been frequently said, Lord Beaverbrook). To add to his tribulations he was reduced to selling capital to balance his bank account; Astley and its outhouses were falling into disrepair; and staff were reduced to one aged butler and a pantry-boy. Travelling was difficult owing to petrol rationing.

Almost all his life prayer had sustained him and now, as he wrote to a friend, 'on prayer I have been increasingly dependent for years'. But it was hard for him to accept the apparent reversal of the divine plan which he had once felt sure he had been chosen as God's instrument to carry through. Accept it he did, yet, pointing to the sentence 'Thy will be done' in the Lords prayer, he once said: 'It's taking me all my time and energy to achieve it.' There were bright spots. He could laugh and be witty, particularly when some of the young Conservatives who had served him as Parliamentary and Private Secretaries visited him, especially his 'beloved' Tommy Dugdale (now Lord Crathorne). It gave him pleasure when Churchill, magnanimous and unsusceptible to hate campaigns, invited him to lunch at 10 Downing Street.

Baldwin once said to Harold Nicolson: 'You will find in politics that you are much exposed to the attribution of false motive. Never complain and never explain.' However, under pressure from his friends, while refusing to write memoirs he agreed that his biography should be written by the historian G. M. Young. This was a grievous error. Young had little sympathy for his subject; he perpetrated errors and put spiteful interpretations on his subject's policies. He did not want to complete his book; unfortunately his publishers insisted that he did so. Others would nail his sly imputations and correct his manifold mistakes. Baldwin's honour, plucked down and mocked, would be restored; but not in his lifetime.

As the war drew to its close, Baldwin's wife died, and the wonderful partnership of over fifty years was ended. He was stunned and his inability to concentrate on a topic increased; he walked with difficulty and mostly he sat ruminating by the fireside. One matter at least improved: he was no longer abused by the public, merely forgotten; yet he could not forget. Driving away from the unveiling of the statue of George v in Old Palace Yard, in October 1947, the crowd raised a cheer, but through his deaf ears he could hear only a noise. Turning to the friend with him he asked: 'Are they booing me?' Two months later, on 13 December, he died peacefully in his sleep. He was buried next to his wife beneath the nave of Worcester Cathedral. In his memory, on the road leading to Astley Hall a simple sandstone monument was built under a beech tree, mainly at the expense of Churchill, who later unveiled it. There is no statue in the Members' Lobby of the House of Commons.

Great injustices were done to Baldwin both during and after the war, but today he is more realistically assessed. He did not halt the economic decline of Britain, a failure he shares with every subsequent Government, and the ill consequences of his idealism about India are still visible. But he steered the nation with great skill away from disaster in the General Strike and the abdication, and he persuaded it to accept a necessary modicum of State intervention in matters of industry and popular welfare. With studied moderation he wooed the representatives of the working class and, as Harold Macmillan says, made the Labour Party 'safe for democracy'. He once said to his Private Secretaries, George Dunnett reported, that he thought he could claim to call himself a Trimmer – that 'this is really my contribution'. If throughout his career he had acted as a George Savile, Marquis of Halifax, he had sought as desperately as the Robert Walpole he admired to keep his country out of war; yet, knowing like the fourth-century Vegetius that those who want peace must prepare for war, he instigated a programme of rearmament and a policy of deterrence. He lived long enough to hear his successor declare war against Germany on grounds now seen to be dubious. That war, as he had feared, bankrupted Britain and destroyed the Empire. He was alive for the 'victory' of 1945 but, it may be hoped, was too old to take in that it was victory only for Russia and America and defeat for the Britain he had so faithfully served, he the mystical businessman from Worcestershire, who, at a price, conquered an inner tremulousness and became a formidable leader of his country.

BIBLIOGRAPHICAL NOTE

Baldwin kept no diary and wrote no memoirs, but during his lifetime published five volumes of his speeches and addresses, many of which are self-revelatory and few of which do not contain nuggets of charm and insight: *On England* (1926), *Our Inheritance* (1928), *This Torch of Freedom* (1935), *Service of Our Lives* (1937) and *An Interpreter of England* (1939). Baldwin's political papers and correspondence are in Cambridge University Library and there is a *Handlist* by A. E. B. Owen (Cambridge, 1973). In this collection are many gaps because Baldwin seldom kept copies of letters he wrote; and personal and family papers are excluded. Some of his letters are to be found in such archives as those of Bonar Law, Austen and Neville Chamberlain and J. Ramsay MacDonald. Among important unpublished papers concerning Baldwin are the journals of his friend and colleague W. C. (First Viscount) Bridgeman. During 1975, one of Baldwin's Private Secretaries, Sir Graham Vincent, deposited in the Leeds University Library a 150-page statement: 'Stanley Baldwin and Re-armament, 1932–38', which however contains only a few new points of illumination. Baldwin may be seen on numerous films, from 1922 to 1937, in the National Film Archive at the British Film Institute and heard on BBC recordings, which begin, how-ever, only in 1932.

Baldwin had two Boswells: Thomas Jones, one-time Assistant Secretary to the Cabinet, whose three-volume *Whitehall Diary 1916–1930* (ed. K. Middlemass) and *A Diary with Letters 1931–1950* (1954) are invaluable, though Jones was not always in tune with Baldwin's political policies; and J. C. C. (later Lord) David-son, whose *Memoirs of a Conservative, 1910–1937* (ed. R. Rhodes James) are useful if not invariably accurate.

SELECT BIBLIOGRAPHY

The most important biographies are:

Hyde, H. M. *Baldwin. The Unexpected Prime Minister* (1973)
Middlemas, K. & Barnes, J. *Baldwin* (1969)
Baldwin, A. W., the Third Earl *My Father: the True Story* (1955)
Bryant, Arthur *Stanley Baldwin: A Tribute* (1937)

Briefer self-contained studies of him are to be found in:

Churchill, W. S. *Great Contemporaries* (1935)
Williams, F. *A Pattern of Rulers* (1965)
Blake, R. *The Conservative Party from Peel to Churchill* (1970)
Crozier, W. P. ed. A. J. P. Taylor *Off the Record, Political Interviews, 1933–43* (1973)
Southgate, D. *The Conservative Leadership, 1832–1932* (1974)
Lindsay, T. F. & Harrington, M. *The Conservative Party, 1918–70* (1974)

Other books with important bearing on Baldwin and his time are:

Amery, L. S., *My Political Life*, Vol. 3, 1929–40 (1955)
Barnett, C., *Collapse of British Power* (1972)
Barnett, C., *Britain and Her Army*, 1509–1970 (1970)
Bassett, R., *Nineteen Thirty One: Political Crisis* (1958)
Bennett, R., *A Picture of the Twenties* (1961)
Blake, R., *The Unknown Prime Minister. Life and Times of A. Bonar Law* (1955)
Butler, R. A., *The Art of the Possible* (1971)
Cowling, M., *The Impact of Labour*, 1920–4 (Cambridge, 1971)
Donaldson, F., *Edward VIII* (1974)
Feiling, K., *Life of Neville Chamberlain* (1946)

Graves, R., and Hodge, A., *The Long Weekend. A Social History of Great Britain, 1918–39* (1941)

Grigg, P. J., *Prejudice and Judgement* (1948)

Gunther, J., *Inside Europe* (1936)

Hardie, F., *The Abyssinian Crisis* (1974)

Howard, M., *The Continental Commitment* (1972)

Jenkins, A., *The Twenties* (1974)

Mackintosh, J. P., *The British Cabinet* (1962 and 1968)

Macmillan, H., *Winds of Change, 1914–39* (1966)

Muggeridge, M., *The Thirties* (1940 and 1947)

Nicolson, H., *King George V* (1952)

Nicolson, H., *Diaries and Letters, 1930–9* (1966)

Oliver, F. S., *The Endless Adventure*, 3 vols. (1932–5)

Percy, Eustace, *Some Memories* (1958)

Raymond, J. (ed.), *The Baldwin Age* (1960)

Rhodes, James, R. *Churchill: A Study in Failure, 1900–39* (1970)

Robertson, E. M. (ed.), *The Origins of the Second World War* (1971)

Roskill, S., *Hankey, Man of Secrets*, Vols. 2 and 3 (1972 and 1974)

Skidelsky, R., *Politicians and the Slump, The Labour Government of 1929–31* (1967)

Strachey, J., *The Coming Struggle for Power* (1932)

Symons, J., *The General Strike* (1957)

Taylor, A. J. P., *English History, 1914–45* (Oxford, 1956)

Taylor, A. J. P., *Origins of the Second World War* (1961)

Taylor, A. J. P., *Beaverbrook* (1972)

Templewood, Viscount (Hoare), *Nine Troubled Years* (1954)

Vansittart, R., *The Mist Procession* (1957)

Walden, D., *The Chanak Affair* (1969)

Watt, D.C., *Personalities and Politics* (1965)

Wilson, T., *Downfall of the Liberal Party, 1914–35* (1966)

Wrench, E., *Geoffrey Dawson and Our Times* (1955)

INDEX

Walpole, Hugh, 47
Walpole, Robert, 147
Walton, William, 80
Ward, Freda Dudley, 132
Waugh, Evelyn, 82
We Can Conquer Unemployment,
  86
Webb, Beatrice, 96
Webb, Mary, 81
Webb, Sidney, 96
Wells, H. G., 81
Wesleyan Collegiate Institution, 2
Wheatley, John, 40
Wigram, Lord, 99, 133
Wilden Forge, 8, 18–19

Wilden House, 4, 7
Williams, Francis, 48
Wilson (reporter), 59
Wilson, Harold, 101
Wilson, Sir Leslie, 35
Winterton, 6th Earl, 51, 88
Wood, Edward, *see* Halifax, Lord
Woolf, Virginia, 81
Workers' Weekly, 61
World War I, 20–1
World War II, 145

Young, G. M., 125, 146

Zinoviev, Grigori, 62